Second Edition

More Than
100
Tools for
Developing
LITERACY

Second Edition

More Than
100
Tools for
Developing
LITERACY

JOAN F. GROEBER

For information:

Corwin Press
A SAGE Company
2455 Teller Road
Thousand Oaks, California 91320
www.corwinpress.com

SAGE Ltd.
1 Oliver's Yard
55 City Road
London EC1Y 1SP
United Kingdom

SAGE India Pvt. Ltd.
B 1/I 1 Mohan Cooperative
 Industrial Area
Mathura Road, New Delhi
India 110 044

SAGE Asia-Pacific Pte. Ltd.
33 Pekin Street #02-01
Far East Square
Singapore 048763

Printed in the United States of America.

Library of Congress Cataloging-in-Publication Data

Groeber, Joan F.
More than 100 tools for developing literacy / Joan F. Groeber. — 2nd ed.
 p. cm.
Rev. ed. of: More than 100 tools for literacy in today's classroom. 1999.
Includes bibliographical references and index.
ISBN 978-1-4129-6436-4 (cloth)
ISBN 978-1-4129-6437-1 (pbk.)
 1. Reading games. 2. Language arts. 3. Thought and thinking Study and teaching.
4. Activity programs in education. 5. Literacy. I. Groeber, Joan F. More than 100 tools for literacy in today's classroom. II. Title. III. Title: More than one hundred tools for developing literacy.

LB1050.4.G76 2008
372.6—dc22   2008012044

This book is printed on acid-free paper.

08   09   10   11   12   10   9   8   7   6   5   4   3   2   1

Acquisitions Editor:	Cathy Hernandez
Associate Editor:	Cassandra Harris
Production Editor:	Eric Garner
Copy Editor:	Gretchen Treadwell
Typesetter:	C&M Digitals (P) Ltd.
Proofreader:	Charlotte Waisner
Indexer:	Sheila Bodell
Cover Designer:	Michael Dubowe
Graphic Designer:	Scott Van Atta

Contents

Preface

*Give a man a fish, feed him for a day; Show (teach) a man
how to fish, feed him for a lifetime.*

—Chinese Proverb

The seeds of this book were planted when I was in graduate school. Professor Steve Hansell asked those of us in his Foundations of Reading class to compile two lists: one detailing ten things we felt students should know when they leave our classroom, and a second list outlining ten things every graduating high school senior should know.

As the class protested that a list this small could barely contain curriculum requirements for one whole grade level in a single subject area—much less an entire thirteen-year education—I realized that Dr. Hansell was asking us to look beyond such limited tasks as recognizing the /ch/ diagraph or counting to 200 by 5s to a broader, metacognitive realm where the classroom becomes an environment in which students are taught how to "fish" mentally, and thus learn to "feed" their minds for a lifetime.

To fulfill Dr. Hansell's requirement—determining what students need to know to progress through the educational system with some measure of success—it is necessary to shift emphasis from identifying and examining those areas where students need remediation to analyzing successful, effective learners and the methods and strategies they employ to comprehend and respond to classroom materials. From that point, the goal becomes helping less experienced learners adopt these techniques, giving them the key to their long-term advancement.

Rather than providing a "tool kit" to fix what's wrong with a particular student's or group's performance, this book seeks to offer a clear blueprint for the acquisition of "life skills" based on what works for effective learners.

—Joan Groeber

WHAT'S NEW IN THIS EDITION

Since this book was published in 1998, educators have seen the unprecedented growth of computer use and the Internet. Preparing students to live in a society that relies heavily on the ability to gather and dispense information online has become a primary responsibility of the school system.

Additional assessment techniques are also included in this edition to allow teachers to make decisions about when and how to judge students' grasp of what is being presented in the classroom.

Finally, a number of activities have been added for upper-middle and high school students. These activities are independent and do not require educators of these grade levels to modify activities aimed at a younger student population.

Acknowledgments

Corwin Press gratefully acknowledges the contributions of the following reviewers:

Melissa Awenowicz
Professor of Instruction and Learning/Director of
   Clinical Experiences
University of Pittsburgh
Pittsburgh, PA

Dr. Eugenia Mora-Flores
Assistant Professor
University of Southern California
Los Angeles, CA

Evelyn M. Kennedy
Reading Specialist
La Pine Elementary School
La Pine, OR

About the Author

 **Joan F. Groeber** is an independent consultant and lecturer in the field of literacy and assessment. A visiting literacy instructor in the College of Education and Human Services at Wright State University in Dayton, Ohio, she has published ten books and more than thirty articles on literacy and assessment tools, classroom management strategies, and self-evaluation for educators from kindergarten to the university level. Joan is actively involved in pet-assisted therapy and is the cofounder of Best Friends Pet Assisted Therapy, a nonprofit group that brings pet therapy teams into hospitals, nursing homes, schools, libraries, and women's centers to help people in need.

CHAPTER ONE

Prereading Exercises

Every truth has four corners. As a teacher, I give you one corner; it is for you as the learner to find the other three.

—Confucius

Every day, students are bombarded with enormous bundles of information from a variety of sources and formats. Competing with the more rapidly delivered modes of auditory and visual communication, reading printed text for informational or recreational purposes is too often reduced in importance to that of a secondary resource for *checking* or *learning more* about a particular topic. Reading remains, however, a critical component in the learning process, challenging educators to assume the task of building students' reading muscles to enhance their opportunities in the classroom and beyond.

Other modes of communication often employ "teasers" including previews of coming attractions to stimulate interest and prepare the audience for what will happen next. This same technique can be used for introducing a written passage to readers. Known as prereading, these exercises provide readers with a chance to think about what they are about to read. Key elements in effective prereading exercises focus on purpose (why they are reading), text format (how the passage is organized), and prior knowledge (what they already know about the topic). In recent years, prior knowledge has taken on greater importance as various cultural differences create additional obstacles for readers, particularly ESL learners.

To gauge effectiveness, assessment of prereading exercises does not necessarily have to be formal. In many instances, informal discussions or journal entries may be sufficient to allow educators to determine students' strengths and weaknesses. A general lack of knowledge on a particular topic by some or all of the class may illustrate a need for alteration in the method and format the information that is provided to students. For example, students participating in a small group or whole class Know-Want to know-Learn (KWL) activity (Ogle, 1986) for an upcoming unit on global warming can provide teachers with information for planning that unit of study. If the amount of information listed in the "K" column (what we know) appears limited or superficial in nature, teachers may want to consider some other activities (watching films or listening to speakers) as precursors to the unit.

Informal journal entries are another way of determining what individual students know before they begin reading. This method is especially effective with older students who may be reluctant to reveal gaps in their knowledge in the presence of their peers (particularly if the topic relates to popular culture). It is far less stressful for students to confide in a journal entry that their knowledge regarding the human reproductive system is far less extensive than that of their peers.

Assigning prereading activities in a position of shared importance in the reading process is a critical first step in developing a workable literacy program for students. Grouped with reading and postreading activities to construct a *scaffold reading experience* (Graves & Graves, 1994), prereading activities must be tailored for the particular student population, the reading selection, and the purpose for using that selection.

To address the increasing prevalence and value of technology in students' lives, this chapter also contains exercises that make use of Internet resources as part of the prereading process. Natural enthusiasm for working in this less traditional format may serve to engage and maintain student interest. Finally, since prereading is part of a process rather than an independent destination, these exercises will take educators' hectic schedules into consideration by providing low-prep, easily integrated options.

USING THIS CHAPTER

Before beginning a unit of study in a language arts or content area class, browse this chapter to find suitable prereading activities to stimulate student interest while assessing their prior knowledge about a topic. Consider your student population. Will your class be more likely to remain engaged and active with a small or group discussion, or is your room filled with introspective learners who would rather use a journal entry to share what they know (and don't know) about the upcoming topic? Try to select three activities that reflect your students' learning styles. Next, consider the type of material you will be covering in the unit. Are reading passages filled with a specialized vocabulary? If this is the case, you may want to consider introducing the vocabulary with a guest speaker who can clarify student questions about the terms or by using an Internet search to find examples of some of the terms in context. Using this option presents an opportunity for students to be exposed to visuals they might not otherwise see. For example, a unit on the solar system is best understood if students first have a chance to view a short film or animation that features vocabulary terms (satellite, black hole, orbital path) paired with a visual representation.

Rather than keeping a formal record of student performance on each prereading activity, many educators prefer to track responses in a folder, noting which format seems to be most effective in preparing students for reading assignments. Another approach is to compare how well a student comprehends a written passage with that student's level of participation in the prereading activity. Students who fail to become involved in any sort of prereading preparation bring less purpose to their encounter with the printed word.

PREREADING #1

Background

Authors of fiction and poetry count on a catchy or thought-provoking title to appeal to their prospective audience. They create this title with great care to capture the essence of the material and provide clues about what they hope readers will come away with after reading their work.

Activity

Ask students to select a poem, short story, or novel to read alone or as a group. Before they begin reading, initiate a brief discussion about the work's title, asking students why they think the author chose that particular word or phrase. Next, ask what mental or sensory images the title conjures for them. Does the title suggest that the story or poem will be happy or sad, hopeful or depressing? Encourage students to share the reasons behind their responses. Next, have students read the work and compose a new title for it. Remind them that the title is the reader's first impression of the material and if it is boring or misrepresents the work, readers may be disappointed and less likely to return to that author for additional stories or poetry. Share the new titles in class, discussing the reasons behind these choices.

Use questions such as the following to help students reflect on their decisions.

- *What piece(s) of information in the text led you to create the new title?*
- *How important is the number and/or order of words in a title in capturing readers' interest? Why do you think this is true?*
- *What expectations did the original title create for you?*
- *What expectations do you think your new title would create for readers?*
- *How is your new title the same or different from the original title?*
- *What role does a book or story title play in your own choice of reading material?*
- *Think of a title that would make a story appealing to you. Why?*
- *Think of a title that would make a story unappealing to you. Why?*
- *Name three other industries beyond publishing that make use of interesting titles to capture their potential audience.*
- *If you were to tell the story of your favorite day, what title would you use?*

PREREADING #2

Background

Readers may have more than one reason for selecting a work based on its title. Two of these key elements are individual interest and the prior knowledge that drive a specific audience to a particular work of fiction or nonfiction. Understanding *why* students read what they read can be helpful in guiding them toward reading selections that will both challenge and interest them.

Activity

Clip copies of fictional short stories and nonfiction articles from age-appropriate magazines or copy them from Internet Web sites. Next, make several index cards bearing only the title of each story and article. Bring the stories and articles to class and share the cards with the students. Ask them to select the title they would most like to read, giving three reasons for their choice and a one-sentence answer regarding what they expect to find in the story or article. You may also ask them to select one title that they would prefer not to read at all, along with a brief explanation of why they feel the way that they do. Then, distribute the stories or articles to the students to read alone or in small groups. After all students have completed their selections, ask them to rank the story or article on a scale of 1–5 based on how well it lived up to their prereading expectations. If the story or article failed to deliver on their expectations, ask them to explain why they were disappointed and how this disappointment would affect their future choices. Finally, ask students to rename the story or article based on their individual reading experience and discuss the reasons behind their new titles.

Use questions such as the following to help students formulate their responses.

- *What reasons can you offer for selecting a story or article based solely on the title?*
- *If you already know something about a particular topic, are you more or less interested in reading an article on that topic? Why?*
- *What is the most important piece of information you expect to learn from a story or article title?*
- *What factors did you take into consideration in selecting a new title for the story or article?*
- *What words or ideas found in the title of a story or article are most unappealing to you? Why?*
- *After reading and ranking the story or article on a scale of 1–5, what reasons can you offer for your decision?*

PREREADING #3

Background

Authors of nonfiction books also use the work's title to stimulate the interest of prospective readers. The title offers a quick, inviting glance into what the text contains. Students can be taught to mine this gold nugget of information to learn more about what is coming in the pages ahead.

Activity

Before students begin to read a nonfiction text, ask them to convert chapter titles or headings found within chapters into questions. Depending on the length of the book and the grade level, focus on a specific chapter or an entire section of a book. For example, a book on mammals might contain the following chapters: "Types of Mammals," "Mammal Habitats," "Mammals' Position in the Food Chain," "Mammals Around the Globe," "Ancient Mammals," "The Differences Between Mammals and Other Species," and "The Future Survival of Mammals." By converting these chapter titles into the questions such as the following, readers can identify their purpose for reading a specific passage: to learn the answers to these questions.

- *What are the types of mammals found on this planet?*
- *Under what conditions can mammals live and thrive?*
- *What is the natural prey of mammals? The natural predator?*
- *What makes mammals different from other species?*
- *How can mammals continue to survive on this planet?*

Instruct students to read the assigned chapter(s) independently or in small groups, reminding them to keep the title question in mind as they read the material. After the reading is completed, in a small or large group, discuss possible answers to the title question. Less experienced readers may benefit from a more structured and guided activity in which the students receive assistance developing the questions beforehand and locating the answers within the material. If this approach is necessary, model this technique one or two times, each time placing more responsibility on the students to generate their own questions and locate answers themselves.

PREREADING #4

Background

Students at all levels are interested in how the information they learn in school pertains to their lives outside the classroom, and students in middle and high school are particularly reluctant to invest large amounts of time and energy in the pursuit of knowledge they consider irrelevant in their own lives. If a teacher is able to identify a connection between a specific topic and the students preparing to study it, chances are greater that the students will make an effort to understand what they are about to read.

Activity

Early in the school year (during the first two weeks), distribute five to seven index cards to each student. Instruct students to write down questions or issues that concern them (one question or concern per index card) as they move closer to being an active participant in our society. Depending on which method works best for the class population, this activity can be completed independently or in small groups. If you feel anonymity may encourage students to be more reflective, allow them to complete the cards independently and submit them anonymously. Collect the cards, sort them by topic and store them for future use. When a new unit of study is about to be introduced, return to the index card file. Which questions in the file relate to the unit topic? For example, if students are concerned that they will not be able to find a good job after graduation, use that question to stimulate a discussion prior to dealing with a unit on economics or career choices. If more than one question is relevant to a unit of study, include those questions in subsequent discussions to further stimulate student interest.

Because the cards represent a glimpse of which questions or issues genuinely concern the students in your class, using them to introduce a unit of study will likely increase the chances that they will be more active participants in any related discussions and activities. You may also wish to construct a "question box" that enables students to share questions anonymously throughout the year. The box should be tamperproof, and emptied periodically so it can be added it to the cards from the beginning of the year. Helping students to see a life connection to what they are learning in class is a solid first step in establishing a purpose for reading the material.

PREREADING #5

Background

Many texts contain review questions at the conclusion of the chapter to help students think about the important ideas in the passage. Their location at the end of the chapter offers these insights *after* students have read the material. Reading these review questions *before* reading the actual material helps students determine their purpose for reading, since the important concepts are often incorporated in the questions.

Activity

Before reading a section or chapter in a nonfiction textbook, ask students, working alone or in pairs, to turn to the end of the section to read the review questions. Instruct them to note, as they read, which part of the text contains the answers to the questions. Which answers were found at the beginning? (Many authors place the most vital information in the first few lines or paragraphs.) Were more answers found near the conclusion of the passage? (Some authors provide a summary statement to restate the most essential facts as an aid to readers.) Afterwards, initiate a whole class discussion on the students' findings. Focus on some of the questions below to guide the discussion.

- *How did reading the questions beforehand affect the way you read?*
- *Were the answers simply available word for word, or did you have to change the wording in the text to respond? Explain.*
- *Which part of the text (beginning, middle, ending) seemed to contain the answers to most or all of the questions?*

If students are experiencing difficulty answering the review questions, break the questions down, focusing on key words and phrases in each question. Are students clear on the meaning of these terms? If not, work with students to identify the key term in each review question, then determine its meaning and its relationship to the concept presented in the text. In the event that no review questions are available in either the student or teacher texts, compose some questions beforehand for the students to use as they read.

PREREADING #6

Background

In the area of current events, students receive only a small portion of their information from nonfiction magazine articles or social studies textbooks. Instead, a significant percentage of their exposure to these topics comes from television and the Internet. While it is important for students to become active participants in the acquisition of knowledge, they should be aware of the fact that the "byte-sized" chunks of information online and on the air often present only a fraction of the story. This can lead to misinterpretation or manipulation of facts. Even though television and the Internet remain important sources for acquiring information, particularly evolving events, it may be necessary to do some background reading to understand the reality of a situation.

Activity

Select a current story on the local, national, or international news arena. The age or grade level of the student population should guide the selection of the topic. Avoid stories that have a short shelf life (nursing home resident's one hundredth birthday) or limited available coverage (coronation of leader in small third world nation). This assignment may be completed by assigning a single topic to the entire class or by presenting the group with a variety of topics from which they may choose one. While there are always breaking news stories, many topics, such as global warming and upcoming elections, are reliable news staples. Take this fact into consideration when composing a topic list.

Using a separate sheet of paper (or a specified ink color), instruct students to write down what they already know about the topic. Then, assign them to look to television or the Internet to see or hear more about the topic using a second sheet of paper (or ink color) to make notes about what they subsequently see or hear about the topic. Finally, instruct students to find and read magazine articles about the same topic. (The school or public library is often a good source for periodicals.) After the reading assignment is completed, ask students to write five to seven statements, using a third sheet of paper (or ink color), that: (1) they did not know previously (List #1), and (2) did not appear in the online or on-air version of the story (List #2). At the conclusion of this assignment, use some of the following questions to guide a group or class discussion.

- *What sort of information did you find in the printed text that was not available online or on television?*
- *Which news source seemed to provide the most comprehensive coverage of the topic? Why do you feel that way?*
- *How did the information in the printed text differ from the information available online or on television?*
- *Which news format made you want to know more about the topic? Why do you feel that way?*
- *Which news format seemed to have the information arranged and presented in the most accessible manner? Why do you feel that way?*
- *How did your prior knowledge (List #1) of the news story affect the way you received either news format? Explain your answer.*

PREREADING #7

Background

One of the primary goals for prereading activities is to enhance students' enjoyment of the material. One way to do this is to become acquainted with the person behind the print, that is, introduce students to the author. This approach is particularly helpful in prereading fictional works as students begin to show a marked preference for certain authors or genres. The Internet is a great resource for learning more about the people who write the books that students read and, while not every author enjoys the immediate recognition factor of J. K. Rowling or Dr. Seuss, becoming acquainted with the storyteller can be helpful in predicting the kind of story that person might write or how their characters might react in a variety of situations. For example, Rowling has been candid about her humble beginnings. The same description could apply to her hero, Harry Potter. And, the author's stubborn determination to persevere despite various roadblocks, along with her seemingly inexhaustible energy (publishing seven lengthy books in five years), is reflected in the over-achieving Hermione. Getting to know the author this way can personalize the reading experience for students. As they become invested in the story characters, readers realize that the flesh and blood person who wrote the book is "one of them," sharing some of the same doubts and disappointments in the pursuit of their dreams.

Activity

While not all works of fiction are thinly veiled autobiographical accounts, many authors admit that they have infused their characters with some part of their own personality—whether it is a love of certain places, a secret goal, or a nervous tic that surfaces at the most inopportune times, making them (or their character) the object of ridicule. Learning this type of information about the author makes the storyteller real for readers. It also gives students an opportunity to make predictions about what the story character might say or do in certain situations.

Prior to reading a book (or series of books) by an author, instruct students to use library resources (i.e., Books in Print) or the Internet to find out something about the person behind the book. After students have gathered the information, use some of the questions below to guide a small or large group discussion about the author(s) each student has chosen.

- *Name three traits, if possible, that you share with the author.*
- *Which time period do you think the author would most enjoy visiting? Explain your choice.*
- *If you met the author at a restaurant and did not know his or her identity, how well (or poorly) do you think the two of you would get along? Why do you feel this is true?*
- *If the author decided to include you as a character in his or her latest book, how do you think they would describe you and why?*

In addition to the informal discussion, many teachers may want to take this activity to the next level, such as having the students do some role playing as the author.

PREREADING #8

Background

Students are more likely to understand, and enjoy, books and articles on topics that are familiar and interesting to them. Their knowledge and expertise in these areas enable them to use such thought processes as *assimilation* (the comparison or two or more ideas focusing on similarities) and *accommodation* (the comparison of two or more ideas focusing on differences) to manipulate the newly acquired information. This mining of prior knowledge is a key factor in understanding unfamiliar and more complex material.

Students gather their prior knowledge from a variety of sources, including word of mouth from friends or relatives. In order to test the validity of prior knowledge, it is a good idea to encourage students to compare what they know firsthand (actual personal experience) with what they have heard, seen, or watched. If one source is consistently in stark contrast with information acquired from other sources, that source cannot be considered as credible or reliable. It does not mean that the information is or will always be incorrect, but students must learn to receive information from that source with the past inconsistencies in mind.

Activity

Initiate a class discussion about an upcoming unit of study by asking students to reflect and share information they have already acquired on that topic, noting the source of the information. Keep in mind that the Internet, once considered by many people to be an up-to-date and definitive source for all types of information, has undergone a number of changes since its inception. The development and growth of weblogs and wikis, for instance, enable people to go online and randomly make changes to the unprotected content of another author. If a writer decides to post factual information on a weblog or wiki to share with others, an unsolicited visitor to that site can, without the author's knowledge or permission, make additions and substitutions to the information, thus potentially rendering it less valuable as a destination for factual information. If an Internet search takes students to a wiki, they should not consider the information to be 100 percent accurate unless the site's author is using some sort of password protection.

This exercise not only helps students to become more adept at using resource materials, but it also provides an opportunity to stimulate interest in a topic prior to reading about it. In pairs or triads, begin by asking students to embark on a scavenger hunt for information on the upcoming topic. Challenge the teams to find at least five facts related to the topic. In order for the facts to count as valid, the teams must be able to confirm them with two other sources. For example, if students find a Web site insisting that less than 40 percent of the American voting population belongs to a major political party, they cannot enter that information as a fact until they find evidence to prove it in two other places, either online or in a book or article. Next, before beginning to read about the topic, gather these verified facts, posting them on a bulletin board arranged by their relation to one another. As the students move on to read about the topic, return to the bulletin board periodically to add more facts, linking them to related information already on the board. The facts can then be written on index cards for easy manipulation throughout the duration of the unit of study.

PREREADING #9

Background

When readers focus on a specific purpose for reading, they are better able to filter the text through this purpose and gain a clearer understanding of ideas being presented. In most cases, the title of a passage provides the primary purpose, or reason, to continue reading. As they read the title, readers should be encouraged to ask, "Why do I need or want to know more about this topic at the present time?" To create additional filters before beginning to read, more questions should be developed, such as "Why do I need to know about this topic in my daily life?" or "How will information about this topic help me when I grow up and become a _____?" Establishing a genuine connection to readers' present and future lives constructs a more solid motivation for wanting to know more about the topic. For example, if a student hopes to grow up and be a marine biologist, it is important for that student to understand that a working knowledge of how ocean currents behave will be critical to success in that career.

Activity

Before students read an expository passage, instruct them to look over the title, section headings, and other text divisions in order to develop two to four questions that they would like to have answered as they read. Encourage them to develop questions that have some relevance to their present or future lives, such as, "How will recycling help make the planet a better place to live?" or "Why do I need to know about how a bill becomes a law if I'm not going to become a politician?" Giving the question relevance to readers' lives strengthens their purpose for reading in search of an answer. This exercise is not limited to current event topics. For instance, middle school students preparing to study a unit on simple machines can be challenged to seek answers about how the presence or absence of one or more simple machines could have a drastic effect of their daily lives. Students or teachers should never regard the pursuit of knowledge as an aimless wandering journey through a stack of textbooks, but rather a search for information that will serve its seekers now and in the future.

PREREADING #10

Background

Poetry is best understood and appreciated when it is shared aloud. The words of a poem act as a great sensory stimulation when listeners can see and hear them at the same time, thus inviting a more vivid mental image of the ideas being presented. Poetry also provides a valuable opportunity to show students how to collect information using all five of their senses. Because students react more actively to familiar sensory input, begin by looking for poetry that contains this type of experience. For example, poems about sticky summer nights or cool spring breezes are sensory feasts that many readers know and appreciate. Sharing a poem with less familiar stimulus can also be effective, yet requires a bit of preparation. For instance, you can share the taste of an exotic food (after checking student records for food allergies) or the unusual sound of a musical instrument with students. Linking the less familiar sights and sounds to more familiar ones can also help students attempt to visualize a poet's message. For example, if students in a warmer region have trouble visualizing a poet's trek through an artic region, ask students to think about the time when they were at the grocery store with a parent or guardian and poked their face all they way into the frozen foods compartment, thus using what students already know to expand their understanding of a new sensation.

Activity

In order to enhance students' ability to focus on constructing mental images, read a poem aloud to a small or large group. Read the poem slowly and don't be reluctant to read it more than one time. As you read, encourage students to close their eyes and allow the poem to wash over them as they think about the words and the images they conjure. Linger over terms with imagery such as "a thick chunk of gooey chocolate" so that students have an opportunity to create a full sensory image in their minds. At the same time, use various vocal tones to further stimulate student imaginations. For example, raise the volume of your voice to read a passage about a chaotic thunderstorm, slipping into almost a whisper for the calm directly before or after a cloudburst. After the reading, discuss, in small or large groups, how the words and phrases in the poem stimulated each of the five senses. Use the questions listed below to guide the discussions.

- *Which parts of the poem were the easiest to see inside your head?*
- *Describe some of the sounds you imagined during the poem. Try to recreate them aloud now.*
- *Think of a time you remember something smelling like the things you encountered in the poem.*
- *How did your fingers or skin feel when you thought about something being described in the poem?*
- *What kind of taste (salty; sweet; bitter) did the poem leave in your mouth?*
- *If you wrote a poem, what kinds of things would you include? Why?*

PREREADING #11

Background

Just as readers have a purpose for reading, story characters have a reason behind their actions. Understanding characters' motivation means examining where they are at the story's opening and where they are by the story's conclusion. Letting an audience in on this information is the author's way of hooking readers' attention as they make the journey alongside the story characters. While the protagonists in young readers' books are often motivated by less complex goals (Winnie the Pooh simply wants some honey when he gets stuck in Piglet's doorway), the characters who populate middle school and young adult fiction may be driven by a variety of feelings, such as love, rage, hope, jealousy, and revenge. In some cases, these feelings are acting simultaneously to prevent the characters from moving forward toward their goals. For example, in settling a debt of honor over the death of his friend, Romeo Montague unleashes a blind rage toward the cousin of his true love, Juliet Capulet. While some prereading exercises conclude as the reader embarks on the story's journey, other types, commonly referred to as *guided reading* give the reader a chance to "take a breath" during the story to reflect on what has happened and predict what may happen next. The process of prediction is a measure of how familiar readers are with the manner in which stories unfold, and how well readers are able to use what they know about the story characters and their own experiences to predict the next major story event.

Guided reading exercises can be conducted independently using preprinted questions that readers consult before continuing with a story, and can also involve small groups where a designated leader poses questions to be discussed at various plot points. The key to developing an effective guided reading exercise lies in keeping the questions open-ended. This fosters further discussion, enables readers to reflect on what has occurred in the story, and think about what impact those events will have on the climax and conclusion.

Activity

Before students begin reading a story, conduct a small or large group discussion noting the story title, plot synopsis, and cover art. Use these elements to get students thinking about what is about to happen, and assign a number of pages or chapters to be read independently. When all readers complete those pages, reunite as a group to discuss what has happened thus far in the story and what character words and actions offer insight into future events. Use some of the questions listed below to guide the discussion.

- *List three character traits that would describe the main character.*
- *Identify the goal the main character hopes to attain.*
- *What impact do you think these traits will have on how the character handles obstacles to that goal?*
- *What types of obstacles stand in the main character's path to that goal?*
- *Which of the main character's traits will be most helpful in attaining the goal?*
- *Which traits will hinder the character's struggle?*

Continue to assign portions of the entire story or book for students to read, pausing at specific intervals to reflect on what has happened and what is yet to come. Near the end of the final discussion, instruct students to jot down the passage that prompted their realization that the main character would (or would not) attain the identified goal.

PREREADING #12

Background

Too often, readers' first introduction to a book is the opening sentence of the first chapter as they begin an in-class or homework assignment. From that point, readers must begin to construct meaning. However, there are countless pieces of information that can be reviewed beforehand to provide readers with a wealth of knowledge about the text's content. These clues include chapter titles, section headings, photos and illustrations, charts, graphs, and sidebars. Prereading activities in which students take the time to investigate these clues can be conducted individually, with pairs, or small groups.

Responses can be verbal, or written with individual students or designated group recorders listing their findings. The primary purpose of this type of activity is to alert readers to the cues they can examine before reading that will help identify and focus their purpose for reading. For example, titles and headings are an organizational tool provided by the author(s) and can be used by readers to evoke their prior knowledge of a topic. If a chapter contains headings such as "Types of Plants," "How Plants Grow," "Using Plants in Industry," and "The Future of Plants in our World," readers can reflect on their prior knowledge of these topics in order to link what they already know to the newly acquired information. Using previewing to activate readers' prior knowledge enhances the time invested in reading as readers anchor the less familiar information to their own experiences, giving the activity more value overall.

Activity

Before beginning a new chapter or unit of study, have students participate in a preview session to prepare them for the less familiar information. One way to conduct this activity is with a worksheet that poses such questions as the ones listed below. The activity can also be conducted verbally with students working in small groups to share ideas with one another. Decisions about which format to use can be made based on the student population, or can be varied by content of the upcoming unit of study.

Questions that ask the student to relate the new information to what they already know are the most effective in promoting a purpose for reading. The questions listed below are a random sample and can be modified to suit various topics and specific student populations.

- *Read the chapter title and look at any pictures found on that page. Based on these items, what type of information do you think the chapter will contain?*
- *List three facts you already know about this topic.*
- *List three questions related to this topic that you hope to have answered in this chapter.*
- *Compare two photos or illustrations in this chapter. How are they alike? How are they different from one another?*
- *Jot down three to four highlighted words and read the sentence or sentences in which they are found. Then, write down one sentence stating what you think the word means. While you read, check your definition against the one found in the text. How close is your definition to the one supplied by the book?*

PREREADING #13

Background

Many teachers already use the webbing method as a prewriting exercise to help young writers come up with ideas before a composition session. In this exercise, students write down a topic and then write down as many words or ideas as possible that relate to that topic. This same technique is valuable to stimulate readers' thought processes before a reading session. In both cases, the critical identification and organization of students' prior knowledge is used to provide a scaffold for any new information. In most instances, it is not necessary to assign a formal grade for this practice of teaching students to cull their memories for past information on a topic. It is sufficient to instead monitor the impact this activity has on the result, such as greater comprehension of a reading passage or a well-developed written composition.

Activity

Begin a small or large group reading session by drawing a circle on the board and writing the topic inside that circle. Ask students to share aloud what they already know about the subject. Copy every response (words or short phrases) offered since doing otherwise might discourage students from participating in the exercise. Continue until one side of the writing space on the board is filled. Encourage students to share what-ever they can remember; their contributions may trigger another student's memory. Then ask students to examine the words and phrases on the board to determine if any connection exists between them. Could the words be placed in categories based on their relationship to one another? For example, if the topic in the center of the word web is "cur-rency," the responses from the students could fit into such categories as "Types of Currency," "How Currency Can Be Used," "Where Currency Is Made," "Materials Used for Making Currency," and "Faces Found on Currency." Ask a volunteer to name a category into which some of the words and phrases already on the board might fit. Write the category on an unused portion of the board, and list words and phrases from the word web that would fit properly into that category, crossing them off the word web as they are recopied. Once all the words are diagrammed, ask students to think of other *new* words they could place under that cate-gory. Repeat these two steps until all or most of the words from the word web have been assigned to a category. The ability to link words to one another based on relationship requires students to have some idea of the word's meaning and use within the context of the specific topic. Therefore, this is a solid first step toward recognizing and comprehending those words when they appear in the written passage.

Remind students as they begin reading to watch the passage for some of the words and phrases from their lists. (Many teachers prefer to write the web and/or lists on a tag board so it can be used throughout the unit of study.) As students read, challenge them to add at least one more word or phrase to each category. For an added challenge, ask students to name an additional category and list three to five new words or phrases under the new category. For evaluation purposes, allow students to complete the first portion of the activity in a small or large group, while completing the two challenges independently as a written assignment at the conclusion of the exercise.

PREREADING #14

Background

Actual reading is only one of the methods available to determine the type of material included in a written passage. This process, while straightforward, can be daunting as readers attempt to soak up all the information regardless of how major or minor a fact might be in relation to the primary topic. Ultimately, large blocks of information, much of which is essential to text comprehension, are lost in what might be termed as *over saturation* leading to "system failure" and ultimately an almost total lack of comprehension and long-term retention.

To counter this, previewing texts prior to reading not only allows students to work with manageable chunks of information, it also accommodates those alternate style learners who understand more clearly when they can examine a work in its component parts.

Students can complete the following previewing activity independently or in small or large groups. For evaluation purposes, an independent or small group format might be preferable. In the case of large group or whole class formats, the teacher can record the responses so that students can read and copy (optional) them.

Activity

Begin with the title and topic of the text, and ask students to compare the two pieces of information. What words in the title help identify it as related to science, social studies, or some other type of text? What expectations might a reader have after reading the title? Instruct students to list three chapter titles and discuss how they relate to the book's title and topic. Do they offer a clearer picture of the subject?

Read the introduction aloud or silently, as appropriate for the student population. Have students, in their own words, tell what they think the author intends to talk about in this book and explain what clues they used to reach that decision. For evaluation purposes, students can write their names and responses on index cards that can be shared anonymously with the rest of the class to stimulate further discussion.

Next, ask students to locate and examine any chart, graph, or map in the book. Randomly select students to tell at last two facts they learned from each of these special texts feature. Largely ignored by many readers, these features contain a wealth of information about the topic.

Glancing through the index at the back of the book, next instruct students to list three to six words that they recognize. Ask them to write these words and their definitions on a sheet of paper along with how they think these words will fit in with the topic of the book.

Keep track of student responses to these exercises and refer to them as students begin reading the text. Ask them what they learned during the previewing exercise that helped prepare them for this material. Compare this activity to other situations when people have an opportunity to preview something before the actual experience takes place (cinematic coming attractions, illustrated restaurant menus). How do such situations prepare us for related actual experience?

PREREADING #15

Background

The more teachers know about the previous knowledge and experience students bring to the classroom, the better they can serve individual students' needs by presenting information as it relates to an existing body of knowledge. In addition to differences in reading levels, many students have the additional challenge of learning English as a second language. These students have a different set of cultural experiences and might also encounter difficulty with the use of American slang and idioms. While many activities involving prior knowledge are conducted with small or large groups to set the tone and direction for depth of study of a particular topic, it is important, on occasion, to determine what each individual student currently understands about a subject. Such evaluations are critical in order for teachers to provide suitable reading material and other media for use during a unit of study.

Activity

To determine individual students' prior knowledge and understanding of a topic, use a cloze activity: reproduce a relevant passage from their nonfiction text, deleting every seventh or ninth word. Avoid deleting key vocabulary terms that are unfamiliar to most students. Distribute copies of the altered passage to the entire class, instructing them to fill in whatever word(s) they think will make sense in each of the blank spaces.

Collect and review the completed papers, noting any areas with a high rate of incorrect response as this may indicate a general lack of understanding shared by the entire class, a situation that could exist for a variety of reasons. This information alerts the teacher to invest additional time to ensure that students' understanding of these specific concepts is clear. Use the cloze activity information to place students in groups for class activities and for lesson planning, focusing on those areas where student knowledge is weakest. Enrichment activities can then be built around areas where student experience and interest are greatest.

A variation of the cloze procedure can be created by replacing the blank space with one correct word choice and two incorrect options, instructing students to choose the word they feel fits into the space.

C H A P T E R   T W O

Exploring Fiction

All good books are alike in that they are truer than if they really happened and after you are finished reading one, you will feel that all that happened to you, and afterwards, it all belongs to you.

—Ernest Hemingway

Mysteries, fantasies, fairy tales, and science fiction share one common element: the author is telling a story—breathing life into characters whose trials and triumphs have the power to engage readers of all ages. The most effective fiction manages to construct a solid connection between its characters and the audience, with multidimensional characters at the heart of any good story. Even the most elaborate plot line and lavish story setting may prove incapable of finding an audience if these individuals are not present. While it is highly unlikely that a school like Hogwarts could exist in the real world, millions of readers are happy to make the trip there because they can identify with the pain and frustration of Harry Potter's loss and the strong bond of friendship he has forged with Ron and Hermione. While J. K. Rowling has done a remarkable job of creating an intricately detailed fantasy world, it is clearly the young wizards residing there who have captured the hearts of young and young-at-heart readers around the globe. And, to understand and accept Harry is to learn more about ourselves.

Fiction allows readers to delve into their own personal experiences, bringing what they know about themselves and how they deal with conflict to the lives of the heroes, heroines, and villains of these stories. The ability, or failure, to identify common ground prompts readers to feel empathy or apathy for a character's plight. In the classroom, exercises that build on this relationship between readers and characters provide a solid foundation for introduction of other story elements, such as *plot, setting,* and *theme.* Once readers establish a reason to care about a character, they are willing to invest some time and emotion in a shared journey. Authors of fiction share the not-so-secret aspiration of having the opportunity to invite readers into the world they have created to spend time with their story's characters.

As readers move forward to explore new works of fiction, they can use what they have learned about plot and character development from previous stories to predict how a new plot will unfold and how characters will respond to the obstacles and challenges they face. Activities that promote this type of prediction foster a greater understanding of what is involved in storytelling. When educators create an environment where students are encouraged to make these educated guesses, even the most reluctant readers can become confirmed "book hounds" who relish every opportunity to enter that special world where characters are waiting to confide their hopes and dreams.

USING THIS CHAPTER

One of the most reliable methods to transfer reluctant readers into rabid book hounds is to give children the tools they need to become adept at story selection. Forcing students to plow through a required reading list during the summer often fosters a silent resentment over the time spent away from leisure activities reading stories that have little or no relevance to the readers' lives. The greater control children have over story selection, then, the more likely they are to look forward to reading time. This way, summer reading can move from a burden to a wonderful retreat from sweltering temperatures or rainy days. The wise educator prepares a comprehensive list from which students may choose a certain number of titles to read over the summer vacation. By the time the school bell rings again, students will be anxious to share (through response activities) at least one of the book adventures they experienced.

Another proven tactic to destroy any natural desire to read comes with the "All You Can Read" method, which likens book selection and "digestion" to a restaurant buffet where excited diners attempt to break the bank by consuming as much food as possible for a single price. Few people approach the buffet with this attitude and come away feeling satisfied. The same is true for readers who wolf down as many '"thin" books as possible to drive up their total count.

The activities in this chapter are suitable for independent reading and small group discussion. While assessment may be less formal than the response activities found in Chapter 4, student contributions to book talks or journal entries will provide teachers with insight regarding readers' strengths and weaknesses, as well as individual preferences. The latter is essential in helping students develop criteria for making future selections.

EXPLORING FICTION #1

Background

The most enjoyable picture books use the text and illustrations together as storytelling partners. Young children listening to bedtime stories from their parents are so eager for a visualization of the characters and events that while the parent relates the tale from memory, children often interrupt with requests of more detailed descriptions of what the princess looks like or how tall the castle stands. For beginning readers, illustrations offer key insights into understanding what the written text contains. For more experienced readers, appropriate illustrations go a long way in enhancing the sensory experience as these children equate the images they see with their own prior knowledge of the world and world of literature. For all readers, illustrations can often add a rich dimension to a good story, breathing depth and excitement into just about any tale.

Activity

Allow students to each select their favorite picture book, and to look carefully at the illustrations in the story. Then, on paper or as part of a class discussion, ask them to list at least eight details provided in the pictures that are not available in the text. During this exercise, challenge students to think beyond the visual imagery the illustrations offer to include other sensory input. For example, if an illustration of a moonlit night shows a wise owl perched in a high tree, encourage students to mimic the sound an owl might make in the story. In a scene where children are pictured diving into a huge pile of snow, ask readers to think about how those children's noses or wet mittens might feel as they make their landing. A well-drawn illustration of gooey chocolate dripping from a story character's fingers might actually stimulate the appetites of many students (and more than a few teachers).

Building on the visual details and sensory cues above, an additional questioning session can further explore the connection that exists between words and illustrations in a picture book. Cover the words in any picture book and instruct students to try to tell as much as they can about the story using only cues from the illustrations. Use questions like the ones listed below to guide the discussion.

- *How does the illustrator let you now how the main character is feeling?*
- *Name three things you notice about the story's setting (the place where the story happens). How much would the story change if one of those things changed? (The story might take place in daylight rather than night, or on a country road rather than a busy city street.)*
- *What four statements, not related to physical appearance, could you make about the main character from looking at the illustrations? For example, you can't say that the character is tall or short but you might be able to see that the character likes to read if you see a book in hand or nearby in several of the illustrations.*
- *Look at some of the illustrations of the main character's face. Can you think of a time that you felt like making the same kind of expression (sad, happy, angry) as the main character? What seems to be going on in the character's life at that moment? Does the incident seem similar or different from the moment in your life?*

EXPLORING FICTION #2

Background

Believable characters are at the heart of a compelling work of fiction. As readers become acquainted with these story characters, they can imagine how it might be to have these people as friends or, in the case of strong antagonists, enemies. Putting a character into the context of the real world requires readers to use information from the story to predict how a character might act or feel about a variety of situations. For example, if a character displays indecisive behaviors, it is easy to imagine that person entering a grocery store and spending several minutes trying to decide which brand of cereal to purchase or deliberating about which checkout line might be fastest. While this type of sufficient information can be critical, experienced readers can mine passages for clues that reveal a great deal more about that individual's personality traits and overall character. This ability to extrapolate a character's behaviors and beliefs beyond the printed text demonstrates a reader's comprehension of the character.

Activity

This activity works well with students studying the political party and election system of our country and can be used effectively alongside a social studies unit on those topics. Small or large groups may be reading the same work of fiction, or individual students can make independent selections. In either case, students will be asked to mine character information in the story to make certain predictions about the political preferences of a story character.

Begin this exercise with a discussion about the major political parties in our country. The depth on this topic depends on the age or ability level of the student population and how comprehensive of a study of political parties is intended. After the discussion, instruct students, in small groups, to compile a list of the ideologies of each of the political parties. Then share the compiled lists in a whole class activity and develop a consensus of opinion. Next, instruct students to select one of the primary characters (protagonist or antagonist) from a story they are reading and make a list about some of that character's beliefs and traits. Comparing the character's traits and beliefs with each political party's ideology, ask students to make a decision about which political party that character might choose. Use passages from the text to substantiate the choice. Finally, imagine that the story character is running for political office, and students must write or deliver a speech (three to five minutes) in the voice of the story character. For assessment purposes, students should be judged more on the content of the speech rather than the delivery. If time constraints make the delivery of all speeches impractical, have students act as the character's speechwriter and provide a copy of the speech their '"candidate" will be making at an upcoming event.

EXPLORING FICTION #3

Background

Readers can learn a lot about characters from the words used to describe speaking, such as "he shouted" or "she explained slowly." These phrases, often referred to as *tag lines*, provide hints about a person's personality: happy, impatient, rude, and so on. Since books are not ordinarily an auditory medium (except in the case of audio books), these emotive phrases suggest to the reader the tone, speed, and inflection that the speaker uses. Readers can compare this information with what they know about real-life speech patterns and make decisions about which emotions the characters are experiencing throughout the story. For example, if most of a character's tag lines suggest a slow or deliberate delivery, it might be said that the character is an introspective individual who is prone to weighing issues carefully before sharing a well-thought-out opinion. Likewise, consistent use of words related to a speedy response might label a character as impulsive. Reading and reflecting on tag lines gives readers additional information about a character's personality.

Activity

Have students select a character other than the main story character and jot down five phrases that describe how he or she speaks. Are the words delivered in a hasty or halting manner? Does the character "spit out" the words or "linger" on each syllable of a response? Ask students to take notes and then compile them to form three conclusions about that character's personality. For example, one might describe a character whose responses are frequently delivered "calmly," "slowly," or "gently" as a patient person while a person who "snaps" or "snarls" a response to be exactly opposite of the patient person. With each conclusion, instruct students to provide excerpts from the passages to substantiate their choices. The questions listed below can then be used to discuss the outcome of this activity.

- *Can you think of anyone you know who behaves like this character?*
- *How would you feel about having this character as a friend? An enemy?*
- *What do you think this character would do if he or she were stuck in a major traffic jam? Why do you say that?*
- *Imagine you are a career counselor. Help this character select a suitable career.*
- *Think about characters you have met in other stories. In your opinion, who would make a good friend for this character? Why do you think so?*

EXPLORING FICTION #4

Background

Skilled authors offer just enough information about their characters' physical appearance to stimulate readers' interest but not enough to squelch their imaginations. Viewing herself in the mirror, a character may proclaim her nose "not quite right" which allows readers to eliminate their own perception of the perfect nose but leaves the door open to envision a very acceptable nose viewed only by the character as inadequate. A character whose classic nose seems odd and out of proportion when compared to her classmates' perky turned-up noses may, by the end of the story, realize that her nose is a reflection of her genetic heritage—a reminder of the generations who came before her. This realization may be enough to help the character appreciate her unique appearance.

Appearance is also important in helping readers determine if certain plot devices are plausible. For example, a mature-looking fifteen-year-old might be able to masquerade as a college student in order to investigate strange occurrences on a small town campus, while a baby-faced eighteen-year-old could pass for much younger when it suits the author's purpose. Character traits can also be modeled, as with a slightly built teenager struggling with, and possibly overcoming, a larger foe in order to stand up for someone or something that is dear to him. This testifies to the young man's resolve to rise to any challenge in the name of this person or cause, and may be contagious in a reader.

Movies and television programs often thwart readers' visual images of certain story characters since the characters explicitly appear possessing a prescribed set of features that may or may not coincide with readers' perceptions. Completing assignments of this nature is less difficult when the story has not been retold in a visual medium.

Activity

Instruct students to create a visual image of one of the characters in a story that they are currently reading. Encourage them to be specific with details of the character's physical appearance, going beyond hair or eye color to note features such as the size and shape of the nose and ears. With this visual image in mind, instruct students working independently to provide written responses to some of the questions listed below.

- *What do you think the character would consider his or her best physical attribute? The worst? Why did you choose those features?*

- *Which physical feature do you feel causes the character the greatest distress when dealing with peers? Why do you say that?*
- *In your opinion, is the character overreacting to this "negative" feature exaggerating its importance to his or her life?*
- *Which of your physical features do you consider the most favorable to your appearance? Why?*

Finally, have students write a letter to the character, offering empathy or advice about how the character perceives his or her appearance. Encourage students to regard the character as they would a friend who seems to need some support and/or advice. As a class, share the letters to stimulate a group discussion about the role physical appearance plays in our lives.

EXPLORING FICTION #5

Background

While many authors and readers view characterization as the primary element in storytelling, story setting also possesses the power to engage and hold readers' attention as authors use it to enhance energy or heighten suspense. In some instances, a character is introduced in an almost idyllic setting only to be abruptly displaced. The middle of the story can find characters struggling to return to that place, and in the end, realize their dreams or realize that their own peace of mind, rather than the peaceful locale, will give them true happiness.

Some story settings share a place of prominence with the characters. In Pat Conroy's *Prince of Tides,* the southern location engenders a host of cultural norms that drive the actions of the characters and allow for certain plot devices. For readers, there may be some question about whether the tale might have unfolded differently if the setting had been an urban or suburban community. The influence of setting on a story outcome can additionally provide a strong basis for discussion of cultural norms and whether there are any universal codes of behavior.

Activity

Instruct students to reflect on the area of the country or world where the story they are currently reading takes place before jotting down four to six facts they believe to be true about that region. What effect, if any, does the story location seem to have on character behaviors and story events? Challenge students to determine whether the story setting acts to empower or hinder the characters. Ask students to provide passages from the story to substantiate their choice. Use some of the questions listed below to stimulate a discussion of the story setting.

- *How early in the story does the author introduce the setting? How important do you feel it is to let readers know where characters reside?*
- *Which characters, if any, seem to behave out of sync with the cultural norms of their location? What makes you think so?*
- *Which aspects of the story setting seem to have the greatest or least impact on the characters? What makes you say that?*

Following the discussion, instruct students to use desktop publishing software to create an advertising brochure encouraging others to visit the region. For inspiration, provide commercially prepared travel brochures for some initial ideas on content and layout. Students should provide an accurate portrayal of the area while attempting to "sell" it to the public. For example, if a story takes place in a small rural community, a student's brochure might invite people to visit or move there because "you won't strain your neck looking up at tall buildings." Let students browse the Internet to find photos to include in their brochure. Display the completed brochures on a classroom or hallway bulletin board.

EXPLORING FICTION #6

Background

The description of a character's appearance is the reader's initial connection with that character and can be the *hook* that gets readers interested enough to seek some common ground with the character. The quest for a universally appealing character is every author's goal but imagine the difficulty of this task: trendsetters and ugly ducklings appeal to different types of readers.

Clothing, for example, plays a significant role in character description. The right combination of shirts, sweaters, slacks, and shoes can spell instant connection between the reader and character; the wrong outfit could lead the reader to reject the character. Sometimes, authors use intentionally vague references such as "jeans" or "jacket" giving readers the chance to plug in information about the current style (wide leg, boot cut, etc.) to imagine a character whose fashion sense they can understand and appreciate.

There are times, however, when the author uses clothing to define a character's decision to be unique. Some offbeat characters might wear something from a trunk in the attic that was popular when their parents were teenagers. This "look at me—I'm different" fashion statement lets readers know that characters aren't afraid to experiment with new and unusual looks. These characters often possess less conventional views and opinions and sometimes suffer the taunts of their peers due to their individuality. This very trait often makes a character appealing, but an author must be cautious. Few young readers will be interested in learning more about a character that scours the attic in search of Grandma's old housedresses or Grandpa's sweater vests.

Activity

Have students select a character (not necessarily the main character) and, as they read, name three details they learned about that character's attire. How was this information presented in the story—did the story narrator or some of the other characters comment on the character's clothing? Then, have students reflect on the character's fashion choices compared to their own, using a Venn diagram to compare similarities and differences.

In small group discussions, have students imagine their characters as members of the student body at school. Use some of the questions listed below to guide the discussion.

- *How would other students at school react to the character(s)?*
- *How much or little emphasis is placed on dress at school? Why do you think that is true?*
- *Which articles of clothing do you think the character would be willing to spend a month's allowance to purchase? Explain your choice.*
- *What article of clothing would the character not be caught dead wearing? Explain your answer.*

Finally, have students sketch an outfit (or cut and paste an outfit from catalog pages) depicting a style the character would enjoy receiving as a gift. Share the finished sketches and montages with the small group and discuss why these outfits were chosen.

EXPLORING FICTION #7

Background

As in real life, what a character *does* sends a stronger, if often contradictory, message than what he or she *says*. Comparing words and actions is a good way to identify characters as positive or negative individuals. Positive individuals strive to say what they mean rather than conceal their true feelings with empty statements that are often in conflict with their body language. For example, a character maintains that he is happy to be at a new school but spends a good part of his time engaging in destructive behavior. While these negative actions may get him the attention he craves, he is clearly not happy about his new environment and, despite what he says, he is unable to behave as though he is.

Sometimes characters make an intentional decision to conceal their true feelings and make statements that do not reflect what they believe. They may assume this behavior with a goal in mind (a politician may behave in a certain way to increase voter appeal; a girl may try to emulate the behavior she feels will attract new or more boyfriends).

At some point in the story, these characters are faced with the decision to continue their charades or "come clean" and let their actions match their words. In doing this, characters realize that being true to oneself is a foundation for being honest with others. In William Shakespeare's *Hamlet*, Polonius cautions his son " . . . to thine own self be true; and it must follow as the night the day thou cans't not be false to any man."

Activity

Begin as a class, picking three to four characters in a story and noting how often their words and actions are in conflict—not with one another but with themselves. Then, as they read more independently, instruct them to follow one of the characters taking careful notice of some of that character's favorite activities as well as most hated tasks or chores. Students can compile and examine these lists independently or in small groups before answering some of the questions listed below.

- *How frequently are the words and actions of this character in conflict?*
- *In your opinion, why are this character's words and action in conflict?*
- *In your opinion, do you feel the conflict in the character's words and actions is an unconscious or deliberate decision? Why do you say that?*

- *If you were this character's friend or sibling, what would you say to them about the conflict in their words and actions?*
- *Based on what you have read, do you feel this character is trustworthy? Use passages from the text to support your response.*
- *Recall a time when you felt like your words and actions were in direct conflict with one another. What made you want to say one thing and do something different?*

Following the discussion, challenge group members to reach a consensus of opinion about why the character's words and actions are frequently (or infrequently) in conflict with one another. What does this disparity tell you about the character? How do you feel about placing your trust in this type of person? Why do you feel that way? Finally, divide the groups, instructing half of the members to argue against characters acting in a way that is contrary to spoken messages. Challenge the opposing students to make an argument that there are times when it is appropriate for words and actions to differ.

EXPLORING FICTION #8

Background

When readers bond with a character in a story or book, they may entertain ideas of what it would be like to *be with* the character or to actually *be* that character. Well-developed characters evoke strong responses with readers whose interest prompts their desire to continue reading to find out where these characters' journeys lead.

Many intermediate and middle school students develop such a connection to story characters that they may speculate about what their fictional friend or *alter ego* might do in a variety of situations. For example, if a student is experiencing trouble fitting in with a certain group of classmates, they might reflect on how the story character would handle a similar situation and think, "I'll bet Allison wouldn't let people treat her that way . . ." or "If I was Allison, the things those people say wouldn't bother me." These reflections demonstrate a readers' ability to step outside themselves and predict what a character would do. These predictions are rooted in the reader's knowledge of the character's personality and are something less experienced readers rarely do.

Rather than simply allowing students to speculate randomly on what a character will or will not do in any given circumstance, this activity, which can be completed as a written journal entry or a role-playing scenario, requires readers to substantiate their responses with at least one instance in the story that leads them to believe they can predict this reaction from the character.

Activity

Instruct students to select a character from a story they are currently reading. It does not have to be the main character, but it should be a significant character to the story's outcome. (Story characters with fewer than three or four appearances in a story are less well-developed and therefore, more difficult to predict actions.) While student selection of characters is an independent assignment, if students opt for the role-playing format of this assignment, they may work with small groups as their audience.

First, distribute index cards and have students write down a situation on the card. For example, "arriving at a new school," "witnessing a robbery," "seeing an animal in distress," or "overhearing a rumor about a friend." Place all the "situation" cards in a single pile and instruct students to draw one card. If the journal entry format is used, instruct students to assume the identity of the character they have chosen and write responses to the situation on the card. A sample entry might begin this way: "I couldn't believe what I heard them say about Jessie. We've been friends since third grade. But if I walked into the middle of their conversation, they'd realize I lied about saying I had to leave practice early. " Then, at the end of the entry, ask students to identify a passage in the story that convinced them that the character would be more interested in protecting her lie than in defending her friend from a vicious rumor. If the role-playing format is used, the student can appoint classmates to take part in the scenario while the student takes the part of the story character. At the conclusion of the scenario, ask the student to identify the passage that made it logical to assume the story character would behave in the same way as the student did in the role-playing activity. The format of this activity can also be varied so students can develop both written and verbal expression.

EXPLORING FICTION #9

Background

While declining to classify certain works under the heading of *biography,* many authors infuse their main characters with a number of their own personality traits and personal history. These novels are often the strongest work of an author's career, as the story shared has been truly felt and experienced. Charles Dickens and Pat Conroy are two examples of authors who give readers a glimpse into their lives through the eyes and minds of their characters. This approach may help authors tell their stories using the protective insulation of a well-developed character who may avoid or repeat the mistakes they feel that have made in life. The amount and depth of detail used may vary, but at the heart of these characters is the heart of the author.

Activity

Begin this assignment with a discussion of this advice to authors, "Write what you know." This advice does not mean that female authors cannot cast a male character in the lead role or that an adult author should never write from the viewpoint of a teenager. Like readers, authors store up lifetimes of memories and experiences that they bring to their work. They draw from this vast well to develop the short stories and novels we read. With this advice in mind, instruct students to select a story and begin by researching the author on the Internet. Well known authors often have a number of sites including one that may contain their name, such as www.charlesdickens.com, and gathering information about most authors can be done through the use of search engines such as www.google.com or www.dogpile.com. Have students compile a profile of the author including their background and any available details—limiting this part of the assignment to two to three class periods to avoid redundancy. Before reading the story, have students browse and organize the compiled information.

As students read, instruct them to refer to the author's biographical profile for similarities between the author and the story's main characters. Does the author hold the place of main character or does that position belong to someone (spouse, parent, child) who may be important in the author's life? At the conclusion, have students design some way to depict the connection between the author and the story's main character. Encourage the use of visual representations such as Venn diagrams or graphs that highlight the points at which the life of the author and the life of the main character meet at a critical juncture (birth of a child, death of a spouse). If the author is relegated to the position of secondary character is a story, challenge students to determine the possible real life identity of the story's main character and that person's relationship to the author.

Use some of the questions below for a postreading discussion of this assignment.

- *How closely does the portrayal of a story character resemble that of the story's author?*
- *In what ways, if any, does the author create distance between real life and the life of the story character?*
- *If you could meet the author, what one question would you want to ask regarding this story? Why?*
- *If you were writing a story, how would you cast yourself in the story? Explain your response.*

EXPLORING FICTION #10

Background

Trying to find innovative ways to tie student learning to the real world can consume a significant portion of teachers' planning time. By high school, students are still reading fictional novels and still required to produce work that attests to their comprehension of such literary elements as plot, character, and setting; however, the majority of these readers feel reluctant to do one more character study. As teachers, we need to document whether our students have a grasp on these elements, so the need for a new approach takes on greater importance.

Believable story characters seem to possess an essence that prompts readers to imagine that if they suspended disbelief for a short time, those characters could step from the pages of the book and into the classroom or a favorite after-school hangout. Their lives often parallel those of the readers who come to respect and understand the problems these characters encounter in the journey through life.

Activity

Begin this activity with a discussion of the tasks facing students in the months and weeks that lie ahead. In all likelihood, at least one of the responses will pertain to attempts to secure a part-time or full-time job after graduation. Use this topic to then talk about creating a résumé "to present yourself to the working world." As a class, check the Internet or desktop publishing software for examples of how a simple résumé should look (students could also do this independently, depending on the population). While the students read, tell them to focus on the types of skills the main character might be able to include in his or her résumé. They might also take time to jot down some of the factual information, if provided, that would fill up the first portion of the résumé. As the students continue to read and build résumés, offer guidance about how to convert a life skill ("I can do three things at the same time and get all of them right") to an acceptable résumé entry ("superior organizational skills"). If small groups of students are reading the same book, allow two to three students to work together to compile the résumé. Once the information is collected, use desktop publishing software to create a copy for display in the classroom. As an added activity, have students use Post-it Notes to tack up possible suggestions of jobs for the character. (A character who loves animals can work in a veterinary clinic or pet-grooming parlor.) Leave the Post-its in place for five to seven days to determine which of the story characters might be the most or least employable.

EXPLORING FICTION #11

Background

In a comparison of books and films, background music in movies allows one definite advantage over the printed word in building suspense. The tone and volume of the music lets viewers in on the fact that something of significance to the plot is about to happen. Upbeat melodies that seem to increase in volume and intensity suggest that the hero and heroine, separated by circumstance or deliberate obstacles, may find their way back together at last. Slow, pulsing tones with the occasional shrieking strings interlude tell viewers to brace themselves for what is about to happen, for they, unlike the story character, can "hear the music" take on an ominous flavor.

So, how do authors drop literary "hints" to readers about what lies ahead in the story? An element known as *foreshadowing* employs vignettes that offer clues about a new or unexpected direction the story will take. For example, the story's antagonist may be introduced in an early chapter engaging in the some kind of potentially negative behavior that will later threaten the protagonist. What may seem like a character's innocent act of demolishing a shabby garden shed may seem more ominous, in retrospect, when an unseen assailant wielding the same type of implement threatens another character in the story. Another example of foreshadowing describes a lonely wealthy recluse conducting a tour of his mansion to a new housekeeper. As he explains that the house has seemed empty since the death of his wife, the pair strolls through a corridor past a portrait of the deceased woman that bears an eerie resemblance to the housekeeper.

Recognizing foreshadowing gives readers the opportunities to make informed guesses or predictions about what is ahead in the story. Readers who fail to note these clues tucked into the story background by the author miss an exciting opportunity to be in on a special secret.

Activity

While any story can contain examples of foreshadowing, the most common place where these "secrets' are found continues to be the mystery. For readers less experienced in identifying foreshadowing, this may be a good place to start by reading a short story to the class that contains some examples of foreshadowing. At various points in the story, ask students what they think will happen next. Then, ask them what information led them to make their statements. When students seem to have a grasp of the concept, ask them to look for examples in their own independent reading. Finally, challenge students to read a short story that does not contain examples of foreshadowing and try to insert something that will allow readers a glimpse of what may be ahead for the story's protagonist. This assignment can also be completed in small groups with students collaborating on the creation of foreshadowing inserts to share with the rest of the class.

EXPLORING FICTION #12

Background

Near the end of the school year, students have read a number of short stories and novels as well as completed activities and exercises designed to evaluate their comprehension of the literary elements contained in each of the stories. In the weeks before the end of the year, teachers can compile a literature scavenger hunt that challenges students to find certain specific literary elements or plot devices from stories they have read throughout the school year.

The questions should be kept open-ended enough so that more than one response could be considered correct, and varied enough to include each of the literary elements at least once. The hunt can be expanded to other subjects by sharing copies of the items with content area teachers who may have asked the students to read certain works of fiction as part of a social studies or science unit. The assignment can also be ongoing during the final month of classes with students being asked to provide examples from the stories to substantiate their responses. Small incentive prizes could be awarded for speed of completion, rate of accuracy, or most unique responses (using stories not repeated by many other students).

Activity

Begin with a definition and discussion of a scavenger hunt and how one can be conducted virtually by using types of literary elements as the "treasures" in the hunt. At this time, set any restrictions you feel are appropriate while outlining the rules of the activity. For example, you may want to restrict students to stories and novels they have read during the past year or past two years. Distribute the list and review it with students. The list does not have to be completed in a single session or single week. Students can do it during the course of a specified period as a long-term assignment to be completed in and out of school. Use some of the questions below as a sample.

- *Name a story where the protagonist and antagonist are related. Identify the characters and their relationship to one another.*
- *Name a story where most of the activity takes place with a single room or house as the setting. Give three details about the setting.*
- *Name a story with a theme of "do not judge a book by its cover" and explain how the story embodies this theme.*

- *Provide an example of a story that uses foreshadowing and tell what event the foreshadowing foretold.*
- *Name a character who embodies much of the author's personal history.*
- *Name a work of fiction that mirrors an actual historical event.*

A variation of this scavenger hunt would be to compile a set of questions on index cards and have each student draw five to six cards so that no two student hunts would be identical. Evaluate the completed hunt findings based on accuracy and ability to offer insight into responses.

EXPLORING FICTION #13

Background

It is widely suspected that most authors infuse some measure of their own character traits and personalities into one or more of their story characters. It is through the eyes of these characters that readers catch a glimpse of what is important to an author. If, for example, an author feels strongly about civil liberties, one of the story's central characters will likely be involved in a career that promotes improvement of the human condition. In some instances, authors invest their central characters with the theme or moral of the story. In *Grapes of Wrath*, John Steinbeck uses the world-weary shoulders of his primary character, Tom Joad, to transport the central theme of fighting against the oppression of the common man. As Joad's torturous journey to the promised land of California takes him back to where he began—at odds with the law— readers experience every man's struggle between doing the right thing and trying to protect his loved ones. Though Joad's character is flawed, he never stops trying to help downtrodden fellow travelers on his life's journey. His words and actions still resonate in circumstances when human rights are jeopardized.

Activity

Following a discussion about the idea of a literary theme as the central message an author attempts to convey in a story, instruct students to select a book they have recently completed for the following activity. Working independently or in small (three to four students) groups, challenge students to identify the unifying theme of the story. Next, have students reflect on various central characters to find one character (or two) whose words and actions embody that message. Then, instruct students to cite a minimum of five to seven passages in the story when that character's words or actions demonstrate the central theme. For an extended activity, allow students to share their work with classmates comparing similar story themes and how authors found various ways to use characters to communicate the underlying messages of their stories.

EXPLORING FICTION #14

Background

Story characters come in all shapes and sizes with their own sets of values and standards that guide their behavior throughout their journeys. As readers become better acquainted with these literary individuals, they can begin to make judgments about what type of activities the character would enjoy or how a character might react in a variety of situations. Mature readers are more likely to complete this task successfully, as it requires use of knowledge learned about a character in the story and application to the real world. For example, readers using information from a story may make reasonable predictions about the type of career in which the character would succeed, as well as the type of job that would fail to interest that same character. While some of the cues that allow readers to make these predictions are obvious, such as a blind character being unable to become a commercial airline pilot, other information is subtler and readers must be able to recognize usable information. If a story character is not proficient at balancing his or her own checkbook, the odds are against that character doing well in the competitive world of finance and marketing. On the other hand, the character's inability to balance a checkbook might not be a hindrance to acting as the funding coordinator of a charitable organization who decides which concerns should and should not receive funds. Recognizing which information is helpful in making predictions is at the heart of understanding the inner dialogue of a story character.

In fictional accounts as in real life, each person has something worthwhile to offer others. For some people, it is the gift of their time and energy spent volunteering for a cause, for others it may simply be writing a check that will fund the same charity. Both contributions possess unique value, but a person's decision about what to give is not based solely on his or her financial situation. Many wealthy individuals stand in the serving line of a second harvest kitchen for homeless people while some people feel that a check is something that can be done without having to come into close contact with these unfortunate souls.

Activity

Challenge students to return to a story they have recently completed to select a character for this activity. Their choices need not be the story's main character but there must be sufficient information about the character so that they are able to make reasonable predictions about that individual's core values. Once the character is chosen, ask students to decide what is important to the character. What does this character value in life? Is the character a person of action or words? Students should then jot down a thumbnail sketch of the story character's value system. Next, have students go online to look for a list of charitable organizations. The organizations can be local, national, or global in scope. Have students match the type of work done by a specific organization with the values and abilities of the story character. For example, a retired firefighter who also happens to be an avid animal lover might be interested in donating time to help an organization whose members travel to disaster sites to rescue stranded pets. A single parent who is also a grade school teacher may not have time or financial resources to help a child advocacy group, but would be willing to arrange for guest speakers for the school's PTO meetings.

Once the characters are matched with an organization, have each student assume the role of the story character and write a letter to the charitable organization offering to assist and detailing qualifications for the volunteer position. The completed letters can be posted on a classroom bulletin board, and made especially apparent if your school has a Volunteers Week.

CHAPTER THREE

Exploring Nonfiction

Truth is tough. It will not break, like a bubble, at a touch; you may kick it about all day like a football and it will be round and full at evening.

—Oliver Wendell Holmes

Students moving from the primary grades to intermediate, middle, and high school discover that the amount of fiction they read is being gradually replaced by a different type of reading material that deals with factual information. This format is known as *expository,* or nonfiction, text. Comprised of words and phrases similar to those found in fiction, expository materials focus on topics rather than stories or poems. Dealing with subjects ranging from the Revolutionary War to the effects of greenhouse gases on the earth's environment, expository text is arranged in a variety of formats chosen by its authors to bring the information to readers in the most accessible manner.

In this chapter, we will examine the five most common ways that expository text is organized: *description, sequence, comparison, cause and effect,* and *problem and solution.* Becoming familiar with these text structures enhances readers' chances of being able to comprehend the authors' message. In addition to these text structures, this chapter will examine the alternate methods such as charts and graphs that expository authors use to convey information. If readers are unable to read and analyze the information contained in a chart or graph, their ability to develop a clear understanding about the topic is likely to be compromised.

Since a growing number of educators feel that there is a significant correlation between direct instruction of expository text structure and greater comprehension of nonfiction passages (Snow & Sweet, 2003), it should be considered a wise spend of time and resources to ensure that readers at all levels can readily identify these structures in various mediums—textbooks and nonfiction titles, as well as hard copy and online magazine articles. As with reading fiction, teachers must invest a portion of lesson planning and implementation in understanding and addressing the individual learning styles of their students, as encounters with expository text consume a larger part of their typical school day (Chapman & King, 2003). Taking the time to identify the strengths and weaknesses of each reader and develop strategies to facilitate reading comprehension is the first step on a journey toward a more literate future for each student in the classroom and in life.

USING THIS CHAPTER

As readers move from primary grades to middle and high school, the tools they need to deal with print undergo a number of changes. In the earliest years of formal education, much of the factual information students acquire comes from teacher talk, pictures and illustrations, or hands-on experiences. For example, young children learn that a large body of water is called an "ocean" when a parent, guardian, or teacher announces that fact either while pointing to a photo or, for those fortunate enough to experience it first hand, while gesturing toward the massive expanse of waves lapping against a sandy or rocky coastline. However, as students move into intermediate and middle school, they learn not only about things, places, and people through nonfiction or expository texts, they are also introduced to *ideas, concepts,* and *opinions* in the same manner. For this reason, they must acquire a different set of reading behaviors more suited to dealing with this new kind of information.

Nonfiction, or expository, text is organized in a format that differs from fiction in a number of ways. The use of specialized vocabulary often requires the addition of a glossary or mini-dictionary at the end of a book or chapter that enables readers to find information about the new words they will encounter during their exploration of a topic. The use of charts, graphs, and maps is another way that expository text conveys data to readers. Learning how to read and comprehend the information that is organized in this way can enhance readers' understanding of the entire passage.

While a young student's day may include many reading activities, these activities are largely confined to what is classified as language arts or reading or literacy periods. For older learners, reading takes on added importance, as it is required in most subject areas.

EXPLORING NONFICTION #1

Background

Description

One of the most common formats for expository text organization is referred to as *description*. In this format, a topic is introduced and described in detail throughout the passage. For example, a passage about holidays in the United States would focus on listing and describing the different celebrations, noting what types of activities take place during each of the holidays. More emphasis would be placed on recounting information, or description, about the sights, sounds, and smells of the holiday than on its origins or how it compares to holidays in other parts of the world.

In the study of arithmetic, students are presented with an example of an equation, such as "$2 + 4 = 6$." The teacher explains the symbols and solves the equation. Next, the teacher provides students with a problem to solve independently. Finally, the teacher challenges the learner to use props (commercial or teacher-made) to create an equation and write it as a number sentence. This multistep process is intended to give learners a chance to move from observation, to participation, to a desired independent construction of an equation. This same technique can be used with helping students recognize the various types of expository text.

Texts written in the description mode make use of all five senses to bring the topic to life for readers. As many books for younger readers are organized in this format these texts often supply the backbone for readers' knowledge on a given topic. Being able to recognize how a text is organized subsequently helps readers set purpose. If they identify that a text is descriptive in nature, they will learn about a topic's traits and various attributes.

One of the most effective means to understand the structure of a text is to replicate it. Descriptive texts contain information gathered from using all five senses; therefore, writing a descriptive passage requires sharpening all of these senses.

Activity

Begin by sharing a passage of descriptive text with students, through reading it aloud or placing it on an overhead projector for students to read along. Try something that makes extensive use of sensory input, such as an advertisement for food or dining. (This can be easily located on the Internet.) As the passage is read, ask students to focus on how many sensory images are included in the passage. Use the questions listed below to guide a brief discussion.

- *How many sensory references can you identify in the passage?*
- *How many of the five senses were evoked in this passage?*
- *Which sensory references were the strongest? Why do you think so?*

Next, instruct students to check online or in magazines for more descriptive passages involving food or dining, reminding them to reflect on how a descriptive text is organized. Invite students to share some of their examples with the rest of the class and discuss what sort of words (adjectives) make the passages more interesting and informative. Finally, challenge students to select a specific food item or entrée and, assuming the role of a restaurateur, write a descriptive text about the establishment's most famous dish. Display the completed compositions on a bulletin board along with photos or student illustrations of the cuisine being described.

EXPLORING NONFICTION #2

Background

Sequence

Texts organized in the *sequence* format have a prescribed order in which the information is conveyed, and altering that order can have a negative impact on readers' comprehension of the concept being presented. For example, if a text explaining how to construct a birdhouse begins with the steps involved in painting the house's surface and ends with steps about fitting the roof onto the four-sided structure, readers attempting to build a bird house using this passage may be disappointed with the results.

While descriptive passages can move the information around without sacrificing its meaning, sequence texts place the greatest emphasis in a step-by-step format. Common texts organized in this method are often called how-to manuals and cookbooks contain recipes that must be read and completed in sequence to produce positive results.

Like a sequenced activity, the order of a sequence text is essential to understanding the material and producing the desired outcome. Reversal or omission of steps means failure for both reader and writer and, depending on the subject matter, can result in minor errors or major disasters. The success or failure of a sequence text is the easiest of the five basic structures to gauge objectively. If a reader follows the sequence exactly and does not achieve the desired outcome, the fault lies with the writer.

Activity

Challenge students to search the Internet for passages that are written in a specific sequence (how to create a résumé, how a bill becomes a law, how to build a sand castle).

Instruct them to write the steps on index cards, one step per card. Then, have students shuffle the cards and share them with a classmate or in a small group (three to four students). The first challenge involves a classmate (or other group members) unscrambling the steps to form the correct sequence. Repeat this with each group member's set of sequence cards. Then, have each group shuffle all of their cards together and hand them to another group. When all groups have a new set of cards, instruct students to use context cues to separate the cards so that each stack represents the sequence of a single process before arranging them in the correct order. Use some of the questions listed below in a postactivity discussion.

- *What impact did proper sequence have on understanding the passage?*
- *What clues did you use to sort the cards into the proper sequence?*
- *What words and phrases aided you in arranging the cards correctly?*
- *When all the cards were combined, what clues did you use to sort them?*

EXPLORING NONFICTION #3

Background

Comparison

Comparing is one of the earliest advanced-level thinking processes children acquire. From the first time children recognize that not every female face or voice belongs to "Mommy" and that not every four-footed creature is "doggie," they are making decisions based on comparison. Comparing old with unfamiliar, or simple with complex, is the basis of developing and expanding our base of knowledge.

Assimilation, or the process of grouping things based on their similarity to one another, appears to be a less complex process since, in using assimilation, we are simply lining up those attributes about two or more objects that seem to be alike. If the objects do not resemble one another, they are discarded during the process of assimilation. When the process of *accommodation* begins to emerge in young learners, they acquire the ability to mentally place two objects side by side and identify differences that separate the pair. As this process becomes more refined, children are able to recognize that although the furry creature that lives next door has four feet and a tail, the neighbor's tabby cat is not the same animal as the family dog. The latter comparison process requires a higher level of maturity since learners must first establish criteria (pet is shorter than child, four legs and a head) and then identify discrepancies (pet's height, shape of head).

Activity

Have students step to the window of their classroom to look at two buildings visible from that vantage point (if the school is in a rural setting, the objects may be two trees or two barns). Ask them to list as many ways as possible that the two items are alike. Remind them to think in terms of size, shape, and color. Next, have them look at the two objects again, this time focusing on those attributes that separate the pair from one another. When they have finished, use the following questions to reflect on the activity.

- *Which list do you think was easier to make?*
- *Why do you think that is true?*
- *How did you decide what to include on the "differences" list?*

Repeat the activity, using two rooms within the school building. Try to visit a room where the difference in grade level and content area is significant (take an eighth grade class to visit a kindergarten classroom or an English class to a biology lab). After completing the activity, use the questions below to make some comparisons between the two exercises.

- *Do you think composing the second set of lists was easier or more difficult?*
- *Why do you think that is true?*
- *Was it easier or more difficult to find differences between the rooms?*
- *Why do you think that is true?*

To help students who may be experiencing trouble generating a list of differences, tell them to identify an item or condition that exists in both rooms (number of windows, color, etc.) and then look at this item first in one room, then in the other. Another method is to list a number of objects in one room, then observe the other room for the presence or absence of these objects.

EXPLORING NONFICTION #4

Background

Cause and Effect

Newton's third law of motion states that "for every action, there is an equal and opposite reaction" and the truth of this statement is evident in our daily lives. Pulling down on the cord of window blinds causes the blinds to rise. Hitting an oncoming tennis ball with a tennis racquet sends the ball flying in the opposite direction.

Texts organized in *cause and effect* structure can be arranged in more than one way. The *effect* might be stated first, such as an article reporting on a tornado or hurricane in the area, followed by an examination of the *cause(s)* leading up to the event. These texts can also be organized to explore the elements necessary to bring about a particular outcome, as in the case of a passage that states what factors must be present for a woman to produce a set of twins. (Cause is stated factors; effect is set of twins.) When examining cause and effect texts, it is important to point out to readers that the two elements are related to one another and regardless of the order in which they are presented, the cause(s) is (are) responsible for the effect. The equation cannot be reversed. (A tornado is a possible effect of a severe drop in barometric pressure; a tornado does not cause the pressure to drop.)

Activity

This activity is particularly interesting with older students studying current events in a government or social sciences class. Instruct students to research an event that is being reported on the Internet. You may choose to limit this to a political event or allow students to choose something of interest to them, such as global warming. Next, ask them to go online or in magazine articles to find the causes behind their chosen events. For example, if the event is a disaster such as Hurricane Katrina, they must research to find the causes behind the catastrophic occurrence. Remind them to look for article titles that ask *why* or *how* something happened, or *what* factors were present to allow such an event to take place. Students who try to research the causes of global warming by reading an article offering a definition of the term will find their search somewhat limited, so instruct students to conduct a simple "test" on a stated cause before including it in their findings. Does the article or passage show a correlation between the cause and the effect?

For example, the poor condition of the levees in New Orleans is believed to have played a major role in the scope of the devastation in the city. Therefore, while the levees did not cause the hurricane, they were a major cause of the overall disaster.

Once students have researched the causes behind their chosen event, have them present their information to the class in a variety of methods. It can be done verbally as an investigative reporter role-playing experience, or as a visual aid showing the event in the center of a poster surrounded by explanations of the causes that precipitated it. It could also be done as a written article summarizing the findings of the Internet research into a single passage. Allow students some choice in their type of presentation or instruct them to use one approach on this assignment and another approach on the next cause and effect activity.

EXPLORING NONFICTION #5

Background

Problem and Solution

Everyone has problems. Some we can solve on our own while others may require help from someone else. Still other problems may be beyond our control entirely. Texts organized in a *problem and solution* structure identify the problem early in the passage. Ordinarily, the author explains whether the problem will be easy or difficult to solve before offering some suggestions for managing the dilemma. Finally, readers learn how to implement the steps necessary to solve the problem. Texts organized in this format often pose a question in the title or as the topic sentence. For example, an article may bear the title, "What Are We Going to Do About Bullying?" or the topic sentence may ask, 'What do you do when a kid twice your size suddenly wants your lunch money?" These questions set a purpose for the reader who knows that the article will provide some answers or at least more information about the problem of schoolyard bullying.

Activity

Plan time for this activity initially and again in a few weeks so that students can check their problem-solving progress. Students will agree that almost everybody has at least one thing they would like to change about themselves and although it's important to like ourselves, there is nothing wrong with wanting to try to do something better.

Have students think about a habit or characteristic they have that they really don't like, such as interrupting someone who is speaking, always being late for dinner, or bragging too much about their own accomplishments. In their journals, have students state the problem they have identified and offer at least three solutions to reduce or eliminate the problem. Remind them to date their journal entries, and remain conscious of their goals during the weeks or months to follow.

In a few weeks or months, check back on the entry. Now ask students to prepare a new dated journal entry reporting their success in making the change. If changing the behavior has been a struggle, have them try to think of other strategies that might help. If they changed the behavior successfully, ask them to describe the process—was it difficult? Did they have to modify any of their original solutions or did they accomplish the behavior change by using those stated solutions?

Finally, have the students discuss the problems in small groups (three to four members) participants receiving and offering suggestions on all the group members' problems and how to solve them. This activity may have the happy by-product of students getting to know one another and better understanding those behaviors that trouble them. This can lead to increased student tolerance of one another.

EXPLORING NONFICTION #6

Background

Charts and Graphs

Charts and graphs provide readers with an at-a-glance way to grasp and retain sizable amounts of information, particularly numerical data. Visuals of this kind also provide a readable method for comparing data such as the high and low temperatures for a particular region, or a recent trend in warmer temperatures occurring earlier during the calendar year.

Unfortunately, many students miss this vital information by simply passing over graphs and charts that appear on text pages along with the printed words. While it is often the most effective way for an author to convey certain types of information, its value is lost when readers ignore the charts and graphs contained in a passage. Devoting some time to reading, analyzing, and even constructing these features can greatly enhance chances that readers will actually use this material when they encounter it.

Activity

Direct students' attention to a graph or chart found in one of their textbooks. Use some of the questions below to begin the discussion.

- *In what section of the book is this chart or graph found?*
- *What is the topic being covered in this section?*
- *Based on the previous response, what sort of data will you expect to find on the chart or graph?*
- *Authors use graphs and charts to convey information in a specific manner. Why do you think this author chose a graph or chart for this data?*

Following the discussion, instruct students to list five to eight facts they learned from reading the graph or chart. Then, ask them to read some of the printed text on the pages nearest the graph or chart. Was the information repeated in the printed text or was it found only on the visual?

The layout of a graph or chart enables readers to make easier comparisons than in printed text. Continue to examine the graph or chart, and ask students to think about how the individual items on it relate to one another. They can then use the questions listed below to make some comparisons about the data.

- *Which item seems to have the greatest significance?*
- *What makes you say that?*
- *Identify two items on the graph or chart and compare them to one another.*
- *Which of the two items is greater? How much greater? How can you tell?*
- *What conclusions, if any, can you draw about the relationship between the two items?*
- *What relationship do these two items have to the rest of the graph or chart?*

Since each of the students will choose a different combination of two items from the graph or chart, their responses will vary from one another. The information on graphs and charts is intended to stimulate readers' thinking about the relationships that exist between individual items. When the students have answered (in a journal entry or during a small group discussion) the questions listed above, ask them to use the graph or chart information to draw at least two conclusions about the relationship between individual items. For example, if a graph or chart states that twice as many people chose to travel by airplane than by car, one conclusion might be that air travel is quicker or that travel by land is, ultimately, less economical. Being able to read and manipulate the information on graphs and charts is a first step for readers learning to rely on those graphics to provide information that will add depth to their understanding of a topic.

EXPLORING NONFICTION #7

Background

Photos and Illustrations

Many readers, even seasoned veterans of the printed word, often skip over photos in expository text in their desire to hurry to the end of a passage or chapter. In doing so, they pass by the opportunity to view the myriad pieces of relevant information that a single photo contains. Ironically, nonreaders build a great deal of the passage's meaning from the illustrations while mature readers often these visual aids as filler, taking space away from the more highly valued printed word. For all readers, photos and sketches possess the power to breathe life into a page filled with print, but only if readers give them the attention they deserve.

Activity

Instruct students to select a picture from a nonfiction text. Challenge them to list seven to ten things they notice when they look at the picture, encouraging them to look beyond just the objects in the picture. Use the questions below to stimulate their exploration.

- *Which object is shown in the picture's foreground? Why?*
- *What time of day or year do you think the picture depicts? What makes you say that?*
- *Are there more animate or inanimate objects in the picture? What reason do you think the photographer or artist had for doing that?*
- *What does the mood of people or creatures in the picture seem to be? What makes you say that?*
- *Based on the picture, what kind of information do you think the written passage will contain?*
- *If you were asked to write a caption below the picture, what would it be? Explain your response.*

Following this exploration, read the passage associated with the picture aloud in class and ask students to reexamine their lists, adding at least two things they learned about the picture from reading the text. Discuss whether the picture helped them to better understand the text. Then ask students to look at the predictions they made about what the printed text would contain. How accurate were their predictions? Repeat this exercise with other pictures within the passage. Students can work independently or in pairs to complete this activity.

EXPLORING NONFICTION #8

Background

Description

By developing activities that help students train their mind's eye to behave like a video recorder, teachers are encouraging them to increase their multisensory awareness. Exercises that challenge students to reach beyond the more common sensory stimuli to the often neglected senses of touch, taste, and smell as they gather information about an environment gives them a firm grasp of what it means to compose a *descriptive* passage.

The most effective activities begin with what students already know such as their classroom or school building. Since the sights and sounds are so familiar, they can focus more attention on the remaining three senses for their descriptions.

Activity

This activity asks students to write about what a visitor might encounter upon visiting their classroom or school building. (The wide variation of economic conditions among students makes this a wiser choice than a student's room at home.) To begin the exercise, let students know that you want them to use *all* of their senses to form a comprehensive description of what the visitor will experience upon entering the space. Since sensory input descends upon us from various sources, the order in which sensory information is given is not critical. Allow students to describe the experience in whatever way it is most meaningful to them or to the prospective visitor.

In the compositions, encourage students to make suggestions to the visitor that will enhance his or her sensory journey. For example, students could invite the visitor to "close your eyes" and take in the aroma of fresh French fries drifting from the cafeteria around the corner from the front door.

Give students the option of setting the tone for the composition. They may wish to offer a humorous glimpse of the school or give visitors the more realistic view of a travelogue. The only requirement should be that the sensory descriptions in the composition are genuine. When the compositions are complete, invite students to share them with classmates. Everyone may be surprised at the unique quality of each student's perception of an identical space.

EXPLORING NONFICTION #9

Background

Graphs and Charts

As students reach the final years of middle school and enter high school, they are exposed to many more examples of charts and graphs included in nonfiction material. While these graphics are often used to represent numerical values best expressed in this manner, political pollsters make use of the staggering effect that a clever use of graphics can have on readers. For example, if an advertiser wants to imply that more people prefer a particular brand of clothing, the marketing department will construct a bar graph where the difference between 3,000 consumers and 4,000 consumers seems extremely large. (Placing numerical markers to represent 10 consumers, the difference between 3,000 and 4,000 seems significant; if the markers were placed at every 500 consumers, the margin would seem far less impressive.) By making numerical markers relatively small, the climb from 3,000 to 4,000 will appear to take many steps. If, however, that same marketing department wants to show that their prices compare favorably with less expensive clothing lines, then they will make the division between $20 and $80 seem small simply by having fewer numerical markers. (If the markers are placed at $40 intervals, the prices seem nearer to one another than if the markers were places at $20 intervals.) Making students aware of how graphs and charts can be used to convey accurate information that seeks to influence people may actually make these readers more informed citizens. Although the information contained in these graphics is factual, the way the graph or chart is designed may send an almost subliminal message to readers about what the author wants them to think or feel. There are a number of examples of this graphics manipulation in newspapers, magazines, and on the Internet.

Activity

Instruct students to search magazines and the Internet for a nonfiction article that contains some kind of graph or chart that can be reproduced. Begin by having them list at least seven to ten facts they learned from reading the graph or chart. Then, have them read the full printed text of the article. Next, use some of the questions listed below for a small group or whole class discussion about how authors can use graphs and charts to convey their point of view.

- *How does the graph or chart relate to the printed information in the article?*
- *What is the author's message in the printed article?*
- *Examine the graph or chart for evidence of the author's message. Share your findings with the rest of the group.*
- *Reconstruct the graph or chart to reduce or accentuate the author's message. Explain how your completed graph or chart accomplishes its goal.*

Students can be evaluated on their list of facts from the graph or chart as well as their responses to the questions during the discussion, and also their ability to reconstruct a new graph or chart that reduces or accentuates the author's message.

EXPLORING NONFICTION #10

Background

Graphs and Charts

An effective method for helping readers understand how the information is arranged on a graph or chart is to have them construct one themselves. By sorting the information and determining its correct placement on the graph or chart, readers increase their overall comprehension of the structures and are better able to deal with them when they appear in the midst of a nonfiction text.

Since the primary function of most graphs or charts is to compare two or more categories of information, it's a good idea to begin by having students think about the type of data they will collect and the manner in which they will collect it prior to its placement on the graph or chart. Graphs are helpful for charting changing trends, such as the rise and fall of temperatures during a particular summer or to compare the average temperatures between two or more consecutive summers. Charts can be used to collect a variety of responses on a single question. The results of a poll or survey that asks voters to name their favorite presidential candidate can be effectively displayed on a pie chart that shows, at a glance, which candidate is the people's choice.

Activity

Begin with a discussion of how graphs and charts can be used to provide almost instant access to information if readers know how to interpret them. Ask students to think about times they have seen line and bar graphs and pie charts used. What types of information were these graphics attempting to convey to readers?

Next, instruct students to develop a question they want to ask classmates. The question may contain a set group of responses (what is your favorite day of the week?) or it may be open-ended (what is your favorite television program?) in nature. Using the question, ask students to decide which graphic will display their poll results most effectively. (A bar graph shows comparison between two or more responses while a pie chart can accommodate a number of various responses.) Spend some time discussing how, on a pie chart, responses that were given by only one or two people can be grouped into a category entitled "other." Give students one or two periods to poll their classmates with the questions and then, using the responses, challenge them to construct an appropriate graphic that will display their results. Display the completed graphs and charts in class and use some of the questions below in a postactivity discussion.

- *On a bar graph, which response is the most frequent? How can you tell?*
- *On a pie chart, what does a thin slice of the "pie" indicate about a response? What makes you say that?*
- *How can the information on a bar graph be converted to a pie chart?*
- *Select one of the bar graphs being displayed and make a comparison statement about two of the responses.*
- *Select one of the pie charts and identify the most frequent response. How were you able to recognize it?*
- *What does the term "other" mean on the pie chart?*

EXPLORING NONFICTION #11

Background

Cause and Effect

The daily newspaper provides readers with an excellent opportunity to view expository text written in a cause and effect format. The stories that appear there, almost without exception, are focused on some newsworthy event. In many cases, the cause of the event is known and identified. In other instances, causes may be assumed or suspected, and are reported in this manner.

There are a number of sources for finding these types of stories, with one of the most convenient being the Internet. Readers tend to be more invested in an assignment when it has some significance in their own lives. On the Internet, students have the option of not only choosing pertinent news stories but also locating one that has local impact or is of personal importance. Not faced with the same space constraints as hard copy newspapers, online news sources are also able to offer a more comprehensive story to readers.

Activity

Have students, working in triads, examine a hard copy newspaper or online news source to find a story of local or personal interest. The topic could be the consolidation of a school district (which would impact students directly) or the employment outlook for recent college graduates (which would have a slightly delayed impact on senior high school students). Check students' story selection to make certain that it involves the reporting of an event. Instruct students to read the approved article and identify the event being announced in the article, then list three to five causes in order of importance that led up to it. Have the group members sign their names to that document and submit it before shifting groups, sending one member carrying their groups' news story to another group. Repeat the process with the newly formed group (made up of one new member and two remaining members) and have the new group sign their names to the document and submit. Finally, send one of the two remaining members into a new group bringing along the news story. Repeat the process one more time.

Send students back to their original triad to share the submitted documents anonymously with the whole class in a postactivity discussion. Afterwards, compare the cause lists and note the differences between triads regarding which cause was most or least important in bringing about the event. Use some of the questions listed below for the discussion.

- *How did your triad determine which event was being reported?*
- *How did your triad determine which cause seemed most significant?*
- *Which triads found stories in which there was more than one primary cause leading to the event? Identify the news story and name the causes.*
- *In what way were these news accounts similar to one another?*
- *In what way were these news accounts different from one another?*
- *How do you think a journalist determines the causes behind an event before reporting it in print or online?*

EXPLORING NONFICTION #12

Background

Illustrations

Newspaper headlines are often confusing to emerging readers. Written in half-sentences and two- to three-word blurbs, these phrases often violate basic syntactic rules. In some cases, the headline's meaning is enhanced by the use of photographs. Examining the photos is thus an effective tool to aid in assigning meaning to an abbreviated headline.

Activity

This activity can be adjusted for use with younger or older students. For less experienced readers, clip several (six to eight) headlines and accompanying story photos from a daily newspaper, separating them into headline and picture piles. Place students in pairs or triads giving each "team" a pile of headlines and a pile of accompanying story photos. Challenge them to match the headlines to the photos and be prepared to explain their choices. As they make their matches, they should list the clues in either the headlines or in the photos that led them to place each set with its match.

For older students, this activity can be completed independently. Show the class a headline and ask them to list at least two photographs that might logically fit with that headline explaining their choice in one or two sentences. Next, share a news photo with the class and ask them to compose a headline to accompany the photo. Remind them that a news headline ordinarily takes less than a complete sentence to catch the readers' attention.

To incorporate technology into the assignment, present the students with five to eight headlines and instruct them to go online in search of photos that will accompany those stories. As an added challenge, they may not use the actual photo that accompanies the headline but instead locate two to three other pictures that help reinforce the story behind the headline. For example, the headline may announce the rising cost of gasoline and show a line of people in a service station trying to fill up before prices increase. Since students may not use that photo, they may choose an alternate approach, showing a group of people on bicycles. Ask them to explain in one to two paragraphs why they chose their photo. In the case of rising gas prices and the bicycle riders, students may be trying to convey that the rising costs are prompting people to look for alternate transportation. The activity can conclude with students sharing their alternate photos and explanations with the whole class or in small groups, stimulating discussion of the importance of choosing the right photo to draw attention to the headline.

CHAPTER FOUR

Readers' Responses

Spoon-feeding in the long run teaches nothing but the shape of the spoon.

—E. M. Forster

Listeners learn more from a speech or lecture when they are encouraged to ask questions, make suggestions, and offer their opinions about the presentation. This same principle holds true for readers. A story or article becomes more meaningful when readers have the opportunity to share their perspectives about the text by participating in some form of postreading activity. These exercises provide a dual purpose for teachers, shedding light on students' thought processes as well as determining whether or not these students have comprehended the written material.

Activities that ask students to examine particular aspects of a fictional text, such as plot and subplot, setting, theme, characterization, or climax and resolution offer a chance to see how these elements of story structure work together to comprise a work of fiction. When planning reader response activities, avoid limiting options to exclusively written or verbal in nature. Many students possess more talent in one area or the other (Maccagnano, 2007) so varying the activities and offering students some choice regarding how they wish to respond will result in a more accurate idea of students' grasp of the material they have read. For example, students who possess excellent verbal skills will most likely enjoy sharing their responses aloud individually or in a small or large group setting, but may have little to say in a written response activity that poses the same questions. Working in a mode of presentation they enjoy helps students build confidence for future occasions when they must use alternate options.

Moving beyond standard pen and paper tests to examine other methods of evaluating student knowledge of expository text offers educators a unique opportunity to tie the material contained in these sources to students' real lives. Evaluations are more meaningful when students can understand the importance of the new information as it relates to them. Thus, developing response exercises that highlight this real-life connection are more likely to yield results that teachers can use for individual remediation and future lesson planning.

Finally, giving students an opportunity to respond to what they have read underscores an important factor; the information they have acquired is worthy of some sort of reflection, written, verbal, or dramatic, so that it can be organized and clarified in their minds. When students are asked to read passage after passage without an opportunity to spend time reflecting on the importance of the material, they tend to lose sight of its long-term value in their own lives.

USING THIS CHAPTER

In the days after readers have finished a good story, they are brimming with excitement about what they have read. They may have ideas for an alternate ending or want to let the main character know that they have often been in a similar situation or felt the same way. It is during this time that postreading activities are most likely to engage students' attention and passion.

Teachers often confide to friends or colleagues that they are as bored with story summaries as most of their students and well aware that many students copy these assignments from friends, older siblings, or the Internet. Trying to find a postreading exercise that measures students' comprehension while encouraging individual response can indeed be challenging. To meet this challenge, linking the story to readers' personal experiences is one way to determine if: (1) they understand plot sequence and/or story theme; (2) they can recognize a story subplot that relates to their own lives; (3) they can identify specific personality traits in the story's characters. Each of these skills gives teachers some idea of how well (or how poorly) a student has grasped the morals and themes being introduced in the story. This information is helpful for guiding students toward future literature selections that are at or near their ability level.

Reflect on the early morning classroom chatter following the viewing of a favorite movie or television program. The students are relating to some part of the characters' lives that are relevant to them. Many of their comments ("I think she should have done this when . . ." or "I did the same thing as he did last summer when my dad . . .") signal that they are personally relating to these characters. Similar postreading activities will do the same.

READERS' RESPONSE #1

Background

As readers get to know the characters in a story, they begin comparing them, unconsciously, with individuals in their own lives. Readers might also compare a character with a character they encountered in another book. As they organize information about the characters, they are better able to imagine them in situations beyond what is available in the printed text. When readers can manipulate characters outside the parameters of the story world, they develop a better understanding of how the characters' virtues and shortcomings affect their choices in their fictional lives.

Each of us is endowed with a certain set of skills and abilities that will enable us to function in life. As students mature, these sets of skills and abilities draw them toward certain careers. The majority of people enjoy doing something that they do well, so if a person is particularly talented with tasks that require manual dexterity, it is more likely that the person will seek a job where that skill is put to frequent use.

Activity

Ask students to reflect on a character in a book they have recently completed, and think about the skills and abilities that character possesses. Next, brainstorm as a class, about several types of careers and what skills and abilities are necessary for these professions. (Engineers must be good at math; salespeople must have a personality that encourages people to buy what they are selling). Instruct students to make index cards for these professions listing the traits required to do each type of job, and display the completed index cards on a classroom bulletin board. Then, working individually, instruct students to reflect on the skills and abilities that a specific story character possesses, jotting several key words and phrases on a sheet of paper. Have students then take their character's "employment profile" to the bulletin board to see which, if any, professions that character would be suited to pursue. Finally, have students pose as the story characters and write letters to the "employer" listed on the bulletin board ("Dear Mr./Ms. School Principal . . .") explaining why they would be the best candidates for the job. Challenge students to provide examples from the book that support their decision to apply for a specific position. As an extension of this activity, application letters could be shared with the class who could discuss why story characters would or would not, based on their skills and abilities, be good at the chosen career.

READERS' RESPONSE #2

Background

By the time most students have finished reading or listening to a story, they have some definite opinions about another way that characters could have resolved the problems they faced. The more engaged students become in the story, they more willing and anxious they are to take charge of the conflict, devising a different, and in their opinion, more satisfying conclusion to the story. Mining these ideas provides teachers with an excellent opportunity to examine readers' decision-making skills and conflict resolution thought processes.

Activity

After reading or listening to a story, ask students to think about the biggest problem the main character faced during the course of events, as well as how that character chose to resolve the conflict. Use some of the questions listed below to guide a small or large group discussion.

- *Think about the main character in the story you just read. What was the biggest problem facing that character?*
- *Explain in two to three sentences how the character resolved the conflict.*
- *Explain in two to three sentences (written or verbal) how you might have resolved the conflict in a different way.*
- *Why do you think your method for resolving the conflict might have worked better? Not as well? Explain your answer.*

A variation of this activity can work well with pairs of students who have read the same story. Have one member of the pair assume the role of the story character while the second member of the pair explains how the main character should have resolved the conflict. Encourage the students playing the characters to defend their reasons for acting as they did during the story. Then, switch roles with the second student playing the story character while the first student argues that his or her own method for resolving the conflict would have worked better. Allow students to explore all outcomes; for example, the story character (played by Student #2) may decide, after hearing an explanation that Student #1 did, indeed, have a better way to resolve the conflict. In contrast, it may be that in the second round of discussions, Student #2 may not be able to convince Student #1 (playing the story character) that he or she could have solved the problem in a better manner. Give students the opportunity (if they choose) to act out their scenarios for classmates to see which student provides the best rationale for taking a particular course of action.

READERS' RESPONSE #3

Background

As readers learn more about a story's main character, they recognize that character's strengths and limitations, and make judgments about whether they would want to know that person in real life. Most readers tend to focus on the character's strengths, such as athletic ability, intelligence, bravery or loyalty to friends as they begin to unconsciously project their own dreams and aspirations on that individual. ("If I were like Character X, I'd be able to handle the bullies at school.")

Finding activities that celebrate a character's positive attributes is a good first step to not only help readers understand that character, but also provides readers with a chance to focus on which traits they might want to possess and develop in the future.

Activity

Have students imagine that the story's main character is being honored at an award banquet and have them respond to the following questions in writing or in a classroom discussion.

- *Why is this character being honored?*
- *How will the character's acceptance speech begin? Why do you think so?*
- *Who will be there to cheer on the character?*
- *What event (from the story) might result in this honor being bestowed?*

Students can design and construct a medal or award certificate for the character including an explanation of what act of bravery or achievement it is celebrating. The medals and certificates can then be displayed on a classroom bulletin board. As an enrichment activity, have students stage an award banquet for their story characters. Act as the emcee of this event with students playing the roles of their story characters as they accept their honors. Instruct students to prepare brief (one to two minutes) acceptance speeches. If time permits only half the class to be honored in a single period, have the rest of the class act as the press corps anxiously waiting for a postaward quote from the recipients.

READERS' RESPONSE #4

Background

Prediction can work in both directions to gauge student understanding of story events even before those events begin to occur. Looking backwards, students can attempt to travel a few moments into the past to guess what might have been happening just before the author begins to tell the story; possessing this ability demonstrates students' ability to understand cause and effect situations. Just as moviegoers might speculate on what was happening a moment before Jack Dawson sits down at the poker table to win the ticket that takes him to the *Titanic*, Rose, and ultimately, his watery grave, mature readers can make predictions about what the main character may have been doing in the moments before the story begins. They may even offer insights on how those events lead characters to behave in the way they do in the story's first few scenes.

Activity

Instruct readers to read the first chapter of a story. These initial scenes introduce the characters to readers and often offer a glimpse of what lies ahead for them. Then, ask students to return to the first page and reread the first few sentences. Use some of the questions listed below to help students focus on the events that may have occurred "off the page."

- *What do you think the character was doing right before the story begins? Why do you think so?*
- *What impact do you feel these activities had on the character's first action in the story? Why do you say that?*
- *In your opinion, would a different action (before the story begins) cause the character to avoid the trouble that lies ahead in the story? If so, what different course of action would you suggest to the character?*
- *What emotions do you feel the character was experiencing directly before the story begins? Why do you think the character felt that way?*

Next, have students write, draw, or act out a scene that occurred right before the story begins. Challenge them to link their response to the story's initial events. (If the character is terrified of water in the early scenes, the student-authored scene could offer some explanation for that phobia). Finally, instruct students to write, draw, or act out a scene that would have led the character in an entirely different direction from the journey in the story. (If Jack Dawson had lost that game of poker, he might have remained in Europe alive but without ever meeting his true love, Rose.) Last, ask students to share in a journal entry what impact the story events had on the character's life and if that impact was worth what the character endured.

READERS' RESPONSE #5

Background

One of the most significant changes in literature for middle school students and young adults is the blurring of lines between good and evil in story characters. In early childhood folk and fairy tales, wicked witches are wicked and heroes and heroines are pure and essentially without faults. The characters are less complex and young readers can concentrate on plot events and story conflicts, such as the battle between a knight and a fire-breathing dragon that will destroy the village if the knight fails.

Older readers still search for defined limits regarding positive and negative characters, but the lines are more finely drawn. Protagonists are not perfect and antagonists are not without some redeeming traits or motivation. In short, the characters that populate young adult novels are often more realistic than the princesses and talking animals of early childhood stories.

A well-crafted protagonist is far from an ideal human being. Traits such as impatience, jealousy, and rage may initially motivate the protagonist to do something decidedly "un-heroic" but in the end, the character makes a choice to do the right thing regardless of consequences. Complex antagonists may have some of the same basic traits as the protagonist yet are thwarted by some significant event in their lives that has prompted them to seek a different path—one that allows them to rationalize their negative behaviors. Both Romeo and Tybalt were impetuous young men who were given to bursts of anger at being wronged by an enemy. Both were loyal to family but while Romeo valued love and friendship above all else, Tybalt was prepared to engage in deadly battle to defend his family's honor. Viewing this Shakespearean story from various perspectives, it could be said that Romeo's absolute devotion to love (for Juliet), rather than Tybalt's temper, was the catalyst for the battle that ultimately ended both men's lives. The words uttered by Friar Lawrence, ". . . virtue itself turns vice, when misapplied, and vice sometimes by action dignified . . ." clearly underscores the concept that within each of these characteristics, as well as with their flesh and blood manifestations, resides good and evil.

Activity

Using the protagonist and antagonist of a story students have recently completed, instruct them to construct a Venn diagram to illustrate the similarities and differences between these characters. In order to list a particular trait on the diagram, students must be prepared to find quotable evidence from the story that confirms this trait. After the diagrams are complete, use the questions listed below to guide a post-activity discussion.

- *Was it easier to find the similarities or differences between the characters? Why do you think that is true?*
- *Share examples of traits that seem positive but when misapplied, appear negative.*
- *Share examples of negative traits that, in the right circumstance, prove to be noble actions.*
- *Protagonists are considered the heroes and heroines of a story. Explain what combination of traits and behaviors prompts you to classify them in that way.*
- *Antagonists are considered the villains of a story. Who is the antagonist in the story you read and why do you consider this person to be negative?*

READERS' RESPONSE #6

Background

Plots, whether simple or complex, seem to follow a relatively predictable path on their way to the story conclusion. Early in the story, a *setting* is established so that readers can envision where the story is taking place and what restrictions will be placed on its characters due to this time or location. For example, a story set in the Middle Ages does not afford its hero the luxury of escaping from enemies on a jet plane. As the story unfolds, *rising action* occurs as conflicts toss obstacles in the protagonist's path toward a goal. Near the end of the story, a *climax* is reached as readers follow the protagonist to the brink of success or disaster with the outcome often hinging on making the right choice. Finally, in the *denouement* the story conflict is resolved, perhaps not as the reader or the protagonist might have envisioned, but in a logical manner. Being able to recognize and identify these story elements is at the heart of comprehending of *plot*.

Activity

Begin this activity with a discussion about at least two stories that members of the class or group have already read. In the first story, identify the setting, rising action, climax, and denouement of the story. Next, with a second story, have students try to identify the same elements in the new story. Repeat this step until students seem to possess a clear understanding of what role each of these elements plays in the plot. Ask them to think about times when they have recounted a movie or television program to friends and failed to tell the story using this sequence (setting, rising action, climax, denouement). What was the reaction of the friend to this fractured retelling? Was the friend confused or simply disinterested because the story did not move along its predicted path?

Once the story elements are understood, use a story the students have recently completed and instruct them to assume the role of a newspaper or television journalist reporting the "story" of what happened to the characters. (The 1996 version of *Romeo and Juliet* includes an example of this at the onset and conclusion of the film.) Encourage students to use as much journalistic jargon as they wish to compile their reports, which will be read or reported to the public (their classmates), noting the importance of telling the story using the elements discussed in the proper sequence. Post the written accounts on a classroom bulletin board and allow the "television journalists" to share their accounts with the class.

READERS' RESPONSE #7

Background

The most effective response activities are those that give students a chance to combine what they know about the world with what they know about the story they have just read. Such activities allow readers to superimpose real life onto the fictional literature, bringing the characters to life in their minds.

Changing story variables is a great way to actively engage students in examining, in greater depth, the motivations that drive and direct the main character's actions. By switching one or more factors in the story, readers get a chance to become the author, making necessary changes to alter the character's behaviors and gestures, speech, or point of view.

Activity

Have students imagine that a story's main character is an adult instead of a young person. With that idea in mind, instruct them to rewrite a scene from the story, demonstrating how circumstances would be different—better or worse—for the character. Use some of the questions listed below to stimulate discussion on the topic.

- *What places would an adult be permitted to visit where a younger person would not be allowed?*
- *How would the character, as an adult, view this dilemma differently than a younger person? Explain your response.*
- *How would this character's situation change if he or she were several years older? Younger?*
- *At what times would it be more beneficial for the character to be younger?*

On an index card, have each student write a new variable such as the main character living in a different part of the country or with someone other than his or her parents. Place the cards in a bowl and hand them out randomly for group or class discussion. As an extra challenge, have students, working in pairs or triads, dramatize some of the possible scenes these changes might prompt.

READERS' RESPONSE #8

Background

Our closest friends often know what we want for a birthday or graduation without asking because they have been listening all along to our conversations about the types of things we like (and don't like) and might enjoy receiving as a gift. In novels, readers get to know the characters quite well by the conclusion of the story. Observant readers note not only the obvious choices, such as a piece of clothing in the character's favorite color but the more subtle bits of information such as an animal lover not wishing to receive a fur jacket as a present. Selecting an appropriate gift for a character demonstrates readers' attention to story and characterization details, and also an understanding of which details are most significant. (A character whose favorite color is orange may be a rabid Ohio State Buckeyes fan and would be happier with a crimson and gray scarf than with an orange one.) Having this insight into characters' preferences is also a fairly reliable indicator for predicting their behaviors and motivations.

Activity

Tell students to imagine that they are friendly with the main character of the story they just read. That character's birthday is just around the corner but, unfortunately, the character must attend an out of town function and won't be here for the special day. In the character's absence, each member of the class will assume the role of a good friend who has decided to send the birthday present by mail and include a short note about why each particular gift was selected.

Students can begin by searching magazines or the Internet for a photo of the present. (Students may also choose to sketch the item.) Then, ask students to each write the character a note telling why he or she is sure that this package will be a welcome present. They should use story details to explain their choice. ("I know how important family is to you so I was sure you'd like this neat digital family photo album and it's in your favorite color—blue!") Upon completion, attach the photos and sketches of the presents to the letters and post the completed compositions on a classroom bulletin board. A character that shares some of their own preferences may intrigue some students who may not be familiar with the story.

READERS' RESPONSE #9

Background

Long before Superman and Spiderman soared (and web slung) their way across the screen or the pages of comic books, there were amazing characters in stories who were plagued by the same tragic circumstances as these superheroes. The gods, goddesses, and heroic mortals of ancient mythology possessed incredible powers, but also held colossal flaws that were often part of their own demise. In the classroom, the epic tales of Greek and Roman mythology can be compared to the modern day adventures of Superman or Spiderman with a look at similar struggles to find peace in a world that embraces their abilities but rejects their uniqueness. Getting to know the gods, goddesses, heroes, and heroines of mythology provides readers with an entirely new breed of superhero.

Activity

Instruct students to do an Internet search of Greek or Roman mythology. In many instances, there are comparable characters such as Poseidon and Neptune, each of whom rules the ocean for his own people. Have students work independently to research the story of one of these gods or goddesses, or one of the mortals whose lives became entwined with the immortals. Students should find as much information as possible about that individual. Another approach could be to have students work in pairs to research the Greek and Roman counterparts of a certain title (Zeus and Apollo each ruled over the other gods in their domain). While much of the information about these individuals is found in accounts, challenge students to locate and use tales that involve the god, goddess, or mortal as a character rather than simply a subject for research.

Next, challenge students to compile profiles of these larger than life characters as the basis for a small group discussion about which characters in modern literature can be compared to these individuals. Use the questions listed below to stimulate the discussion.

- *What is the character's greatest strength? How does the character use this power in dealing with others?*
- *What is the character's greatest weakness? How does this flaw affect the way in which the character relates to others?*
- *Compare this character to a modern day character. How are they alike? How are they different?*

- *Greek and Roman mythology is filled with tragic scenarios. Explain the tragedy involving the character you chose and whether it might have been avoided.*

Have students share their character profiles with the rest of the group or class, focusing on finding comparisons within that set of characters.

READERS' RESPONSE #10

Background

Story characters do not exist in a vacuum. They travel to a number of locations, encountering people along the way who, in some way, affect the outcome of the story. The character may dread some places in the story and feel safe and secure in others.

Charting the travels of the main character involves a certain amount of sequencing skills, as what happens at one location may cause the character to choose whether to travel to a new setting. In addition, the location of the main character at any given time in the story offers valuable insights into how that character feels at that moment.

Activity

Once students have completed a novel or short story, have them draw a map of the places the main character travels throughout the story. This activity can be done by hand or with the aid of desktop publishing software that allows students to illustrate a map. The annotated map should include labeled locations—such as a school building, hospital, or mall (with full names, if provided)—that the character visits. In constructing the map, students should try to identify as many street names as possible to develop a more comprehensive graphic. The map should indicate the starting location of the story as well as where the story concludes. Before students complete construction of their maps, use some of the following questions to stimulate a discussion.

- *Where does the character begin the story's journey?*
- *List three significant stops the character makes in the course of the journey.*
- *Why do you consider the stops named above to be significant?*
- *Where does the story conclude for the character?*
- *How near or far is that location from the beginning of the story?*

Next, initiate a discussion about map legends and keys and how they are used to let readers know more about a particular location (a target marking designates a city as the state capital; an airplane identifies where an airport is located; trees may be used to denote the location of a state or national preserve).

Challenge students to develop a key for the map that reflects the characters' emotions while traveling through the story map. For example, a glowing yellow sun could be used to identify a place where the character feels safe and secure. Storm clouds could be a place that the character dreads. Following the discussion, have students design icons for a range of emotions such as happy, sad, scared, proud, or uncertain—or a range of emotions that is appropriate for the story. Students should label the map using these icons and include a key on one corner of the map. Display the maps on a classroom or hallway bulletin board.

READERS' RESPONSE #11

Background

Dialogue, monologue, and behaviors are great ways for authors to introduce their characters to readers. In some cases, the three areas are not in total agreement, and this also provides information about the character. For example, characters that say one thing and do the opposite may be insincere or simply afraid to say what they are feeling due to peer pressure. A well-developed character may have these inconsistencies but there is always a reason behind it. Mature readers are able to gather the information and sort through it for these inconsistencies before deciding what type of personality the character may possess. Additional patterns can be revealed by considering how certain characters may display consistent dialogue and behaviors with some of the other characters but not with others. This can indicate which characters the main character considers as friends.

Activity

After completing a novel, instruct students to develop a profile of the main character or a significant secondary character. The profile should include at least five personality traits about that character. Next, have students locate quotes that confirm their selections, and jot these down on a sheet of paper. After the quote search, have students repeat the process, this time looking for passages containing character behaviors that support the notion that the character possesses a certain trait. Scan the book for inconsistencies between the character's words, thoughts (*monologue*), and behaviors and use some of the questions below to stimulate a discussion.

- *What is happening in the character's life when these types of inconsistencies occur?*
- *How do other characters react to these inconsistencies, or do they fail to notice them at all?*
- *What is happening in the character's life when speech, thought, and actions appear to be in harmony with one another? Why do you think that is true?*

Following the discussion, instruct students to complete their profiles of the story character including their opinions regarding any inconsistencies in the character's speech, thoughts, and actions and what it says about the character. This assignment can be completed as a journal entry.

READERS' RESPONSE #12

Background

While fictional stories recount events that are not necessarily true, the story's main event still exists as "fact" for its characters (and for readers, who have suspended their disbelief upon entering this world). This fact lies at the center of the story's plot. Learning as much as possible about the story's primary conflict enables readers to combine their knowledge of story and of the world to make predictions about how each of the characters will react, and, contemplate whether there is any hope for the major players in the drama to resolve the conflict.

Journalists provide a glimpse into the lives of others for their readers and viewers. Entrusted with this task, they must also bear the responsibility of doing so in a way that demonstrates respect for the subject and the audience. Many news outlets treat their subjects like an inanimate object to be poked, prodded, or analyzed while other news sources fail to give their audience credit for making any decisions regarding the quality of the content they are receiving. This second group believes that their "public" will believe, without question, anything they report.

Activity

Initiate a brief discussion about credible journalism and how a free press has a duty to report the news in a responsible manner, while also working on a deadline and within a specified amount of time and space. Stress the importance of reporting accurately and being able to verify what has been written or spoken about another person.

Next, have students select an event that takes place in a story they have just read. The story should be at least important enough to be considered newsworthy whether the news is good or bad. Have students use story details to verify the information they share in the account keeping in mind the six questions that reporters use to organize their stories (who, what, where, when, how, why). Remind students that an exciting headline will make readers want to see what they have to say. Give students a specified time (within a single class period) and amount of space (one to two columns using a desktop publishing software program) to submit their accounts to underscore that papers run on a deadline and must include as much news as possible in a single edition.

For a variation, invite students to become news anchors or on-location reporters who share their information with a listening audience. Students can be given the option of submitting their stories in either format.

Following this exercise, initiate a discussion about how time and space constraints prompt journalists to make certain decisions. Use some of the questions below to guide the discussion.

- *What effect do time and space have on how an article is written?*
- *What effect did time and space have on your article?*
- *How did you decide which details to include or omit in your article?*
- *Why did you choose a particular sentence to begin your article?*
- *What prompted you to use the words in your headline?*

READERS' RESPONSE #13

Background

As teachers search for ways to make instruction and assessment more effective for learners with alternate styles, they must examine activities suited for the auditory learner. The ability of auditory learners to receive, process, and generate information increases greatly when they are permitted to complete these tasks verbally. For example, an auditory learner retains more of a story when the teacher reads it aloud than when the student must read it silently. These students also prefer to answer questions verbally and receive verbal feedback from the teacher rather than write their responses.

Many times, these students have a solid grasp of the concepts being presented but little or no idea of how to organize their thoughts on paper. Because of this, they often perform poorly on written evaluations. Likewise, students accustomed primarily to the written and visual arenas often stumble over the simplest verbal task and experience great anxiety when faced with a verbal classroom presentation.

Keeping a healthy balance of written and verbal activities in the classroom gives students who do not perform as well in traditional modes of expression an opportunity to shine and promotes a more well-rounded learning style in all students.

Activity

Everyone has an internalized notion of what qualities make a good friend and, in general, people gravitate toward other people who possess all, or at least some, of those same qualities.

After students, as a class or in small groups, have finished reading a story, discuss the main character. What sort of traits does that character possess? Students should be prepared to cite instances in the text to support their response. Develop a consensus profile of the main character.

Next, have students reflect on their own criteria for a friend. What sorts of behaviors prompt them to think that someone would make a worthwhile companion? Using a written response, group discussion, or dramatization, have students share why they would (or would not) like to have the story's main character as their friend. During the discussion, stress that while there may be some key behaviors (loyalty, honesty) that may be desirable in all friends, individual choices of friends may differ due to a person's personality. For example, athletic students may find that the main character, also athletic, would make a good friend while a computer devotee might not agree. This discussion provides a good opportunity to discuss that different is often just different—not good or bad—and can be determined by individual taste.

READERS' RESPONSE #14

Background

Readers can respond to a story in many ways. One of the most interesting and exciting methods is through role playing. Assuming the roles of story characters, readers can act out how they think the characters would act when faced with a variety of situations. The simplest form of role playing brings a group of students together on stage to recreate a scene from the story. More creative ventures place the story characters in completely new situations where the actors must use what they know about those characters to face their dilemmas. Teachers can create role-playing scenarios but it's often more fun to let students take an active role in guiding the impromptu productions. Many times, their ideas and performances exceed a teacher's wildest imaginings as they take an invested interest in the learning process.

Activity

Have students focus on the main characters of a story they've read in class recently. Then, have them try one or more of the following scenarios featuring the story characters. When they have completed these scenarios, challenge them to create their own role-playing scenes.

- *Choose a scene in the story where the character must make a decision or take some sort of action. Pretend to be that character and defend your actions to a parent, teacher, or friends. (Roles: main character, parent, teacher, or friend)*
- *Imagine you're the story character and a genie has appeared and offered to grant you a single wish. What will you wish for and why do you want it? (Roles: main character, genie)*
- *Your best friend, the story's main character, is missing and you're very concerned. Give the police a detailed description of the character as well as the names of at least three places where the officer can begin the search. Be sure to tell the officer why you're so concerned. (Roles: main character's best friend, police officer)*
- *Imagine you're a tour guide. Tell your customers all about the wonderful spot (the story setting) they've chosen for their vacation. Let them in on a few of the location's secrets. (Roles: tour guide, vacationers)*

READERS' RESPONSE #15

Background

Whether reading a novel or watching a film, readers and viewers often find themselves thinking, "This heroine sure reminds me of a character from another story." The primary reason for feeling this way can be attributed to the fact that the similar characters are espousing the same literary theme in their words and actions. In L. Frank Baum's turn of the century work, *The Wizard of Oz*, young Dorothy learns through her subconscious journey that there is no place like home as she comes to appreciate her place in the universe. Years later, John Irving's Homer Wells from *The Cider House Rules* experiences the same realization as he travels far from his childhood orphanage home only to discover that his future path may be not far from where he began life. As readers encounter more and more characters, they are likely to find that many of their literary acquaintances reach similar destinations despite a variety of experiences along the way. Recognizing the similarities that exist between these characters' messages demonstrates readers' ability to recognize literary themes but also to identify them in whatever manner they are distilled.

Activity

During the course of many junior and senior literature classes, students are required to read a number of short stories and novels. While genres may vary, readers will encounter many protagonists who embody similar literary themes, such as "love conquers all," "be true to yourself," or "wherever you go, there you are." Instruct students to keep a running record of some sort (card file, informal journal) about the various characters they meet in stories and what these characters are trying to tell readers. At specified periods during the semester or school year, have students take a step back and review their literary acquaintances, examining similarities and differences among them. Use some of the questions listed below to guide a small or large group discussion.

- *Name two characters in literature that embody similar themes. Explain your answer.*
- *Of the two characters, which one do you feel stays truer to the theme? Why do you say that?*
- *Compare the way in which each of the two characters expresses the story's theme (words and actions). Which method do you feel is more effective? Explain your answer.*

- *How would the values and beliefs of these two characters be affected by today's society? Explain your answer.*

Instruct students to find a method for consolidating the discussion answers into some sort of presentation. It could be verbal (debate) or written (Venn diagram) in nature and should include evidence of the similarities and differences of the two characters who share a common literary theme.

READERS' RESPONSE #16

Background

Story setting is often regarded as a passive literary element since it can neither speak nor interact with story characters. However, nothing could be further from the truth. In many stories, the mere fact that characters reside in a specific location has a great deal of bearing on how they conduct themselves and in the choices they make in life. Encouraging students to take note of the places where the story unfolds provides one more way for readers to become actively involved in the lives of the characters. For example, a rural setting may restrict characters' worldliness but may present numerous opportunities for them to build self-reliance in a less complex environment. Such places may even beckon urban dwelling readers to long for a simpler existence. To a greater or lesser extent, story characters are the product of their environment, and understanding that environment means a greater comprehension of those characters.

Activity

Ask students to choose a novel they have recently read. Following a brief discussion on how travel agencies use descriptive phrases and images to entice people to visit specific locations, have students reflect on the primary locations of the story they have just read. What aspects of the setting would most people find appealing? What are the positive attributes of the story setting? Using these ideas as guidelines, instruct students to use desktop publishing software to design and print a brochure describing the story setting and why it would be a great idea to travel there. If the story location does not seem idyllic, challenge students to become "super salespeople" and try to shine a positive light on its attributes. For example, an isolated rural location may have been bad news for a group of overly curious vacationing college students, but for a writer looking for a quiet place to write a novel, the setting may be perfect. Encourage students to identify their audience and market the brochure to them, trying to reach as broad a population as possible. Upon completion, share the completed brochures on a hallway bulletin board. Using a map and yarn to connect a brochure to the place on the map where the story takes place can enhance the display.

CHAPTER FIVE

Note-Taking Strategies for Students

Next to the originator of a great sentence is the first quoter of it.

—Ralph Waldo Emerson

I magine trying to study for a test using the notes of a friend who tried to copy a lecture word for word. Then, try to imagine using the notes from another friend who copied only an abbreviated, shorthand version of a few key vocabulary terms with no information about how these words relate to the topic being discussed. How would this affect your study?

Many students (and some teachers) may not realize it, but taking lecture notes is a skill, and like all skills, it requires organization and practice. But before students are willing to invest the time and energy in taking usable notes, they must recognize the value of this study tool. The very act of note taking, if done properly, can actually increase students' chances of understanding the material and performing well on a written evaluation. There are three primary factors that have the greatest impact on students' ability to take effective notes during a lecture or presentation.

Listening skills: The ability to focus attention and block out most other distractions makes note taking much easier. Good listening requires practice, too, so becoming a good note taker begins with becoming a good listener.

Note organization: Good notes group concepts according to how they relate to each other as well as to the main topic. Knowing beforehand how a speaker has organized the information to be shared is a first step in producing notes that reflect that format.

Note review and test preparation: Even the most effectively organized notes are of little value if students fail to revisit them periodically (rather than the evening before an examination) to refresh and clarify their understanding of the material.

While a number of note-taking strategies exist, Walter Pauk of Cornell University devised a plan (Pauk, 2000) that has weathered the test of time. His method, The Cornell Note Taking System, builds in tools that enable students to organize notes at the time they are taken and return to those pages for study sessions and exam preparation. Even if a student tries and subsequently rejects the Cornell System for personal use, it is critical to help students find a way to take and organize notes for future use. This skill, coupled with effective listening behaviors and solid study habits, form the basis of a successful school career.

USING THIS CHAPTER

While the strategies in this chapter are intended for student use rather than teacher presentation, there are also some techniques that teachers can use in organizing their lectures that will help students become proficient note takers. Although it is advisable that students do the majority of their note review independently, most likely at home, modeling appropriate note review in class will guide students in the right direction and hopefully, convince them of the value of this practice.

While Walter Pauk's Cornell System is probably the most well-known and commonly used version of note organization, there are a number of Web sites that offer tips for students of all grade levels to get the most from their lecture and reading notes. Rather than randomly surfing the Internet in search of these sites, try using a search engine like Google, Dogpile, or Yahoo with the search keyword phrase, "note-taking strategies" to locate some of this extremely useful information. While teaching students how to take and use good notes on their own, try also to set a small amount of classroom instruction time aside to teach this valuable skill.

NOTE-TAKING STRATEGY #1

Background

There are a number of effective note-taking strategies that students can use, but few of them are of value if students cannot learn to focus their attention on the speaker during the lecture. Like note taking, listening is a skill, yet direct instruction in this area is often overlooked due to time constraints. The fact is that if a student isn't actively listening (rather than simply hearing the information without intent), the chance of taking useable notes is not a likely outcome.

A number of factors affect students' ability to listen with understanding to what they hear, including their environment. An uncluttered workspace and sufficient paper for taking notes are essential components. Developing good listening behaviors, such as not interrupting and looking directly at the speakers, and asking relevant questions at the conclusion of a presentation are also valuable tools that will ultimately facilitate better note-taking skills.

Activity

Ask students to write briefly about why, or why not, they think they are good listeners. To conduct this questionnaire, have students number a blank paper from 1 to 9 and respond to each statement as it is read aloud. Read these directions aloud as well: "Write a 2 if you always agree or almost always agree with the statement; write a 1 if you sometimes agree, and write a 0 if you almost never agree with the statement." This entire assignment should be conducted verbally, requiring students to listen to what you say—thus underscoring the importance of developing better listening behaviors in order to absorb material delivered in verbal format.

When you finish reading all nine of the statements in this activity, ask students to total their points. Then, with totals in mind, discuss the questions and their responses. Were they surprised at their scores? Have them compare their results with the statement they initially wrote about their listening skills (at the onset of the activity) and discuss any disparity between them. Finally, ask students to pick one of the statements where they marked 10 or 0 and concentrate on improving that skill during the next week. At the end of the week, have students write a journal entry about how they tried to change their behavior and how well the strategies they employed worked.

Listening Questionnaire

1 I sit up straight and face the speaker.

2 I remove all unnecessary items from my desktop before the speaker begins.

3 I avoid looking at others in the class during a speech or lecture.

4 I think about how this information relates to what I already know on the topic.

5 I try to visualize what the speaker is describing.

6 I make notes of questions I want to ask at the end of the speech.

7 I don't interrupt or talk to others during the speech or lecture.

8 I wait until it is my turn to ask questions following the speech.

9 I ask questions that will increase my understanding of the topic.

Scoring: 15–18 "Ears" to you—you're a first class listener

10–14 Better stay tuned: you may be missing something important

0–9 Listen up!

NOTE-TAKING STRATEGY #2

Background

Younger students often benefit from practicing a skill such as listening by participating in a game or informal activity. Even the most reluctant learner is likely to become actively involved and may enjoy a level of achievement beyond expectations due to the shift in format. These games can be played at various intervals throughout the week and are a great way to reduce disruptive chatter at the end of a school day, or while waiting for the arrival of a bus for a student field trip.

Activity

Begin this listening chain with the phrase, "I went to the mall and bought . . ." completing the sentence with an item purchased such as a DVD. Call on students randomly, and more than once, challenge them to add their "purchases" to the steadily growing shopping list as they repeat aloud each item mentioned to that point in the game and in the correct sequence before adding their own new item. Continue moving around the room to select students, challenging everyone to listen since they may be called upon a second (or third) time. Students cannot help one another with the recounting of the list. A designated recorder (possibly a student teacher, classroom aide or room parent) can sit in one corner of the room keeping track of the "purchases" while the students continue to add to the list. The entire class will become involved in the activity and are likely to recognize a mistake almost immediately.

While this topic (shopping mall) is a great way to get students involved because it provides an opportunity to talk about things they enjoy outside the classroom, this exercise can also be used in connection with classroom subjects. For example, tailor this activity to a particular unit of study by altering the opening phrase: I drove across America and visited the state of _____ whose capital is _____. It can also be used following a field trip (on the bus or at school the following day) to recount the things students saw or experienced on the trip.

NOTE-TAKING STRATEGY #3

Background

In middle and high school, a significant portion of the school day is spent listening to lecturers and other verbal presentations, placing a critical role on developing good listening skills. Unfortunately, many students fail to listen and rely instead on the fact that many teachers will provide some sort of related handout at the onset or conclusion of the lecture. While this is a wise practice to reinforce the major points of a lecture, students miss an opportunity to fine tune their listening skills because they can always refer to the handout. Removing the handout occasionally is a solid first step in prompting students to sharpen their listening skills for those times when no handout is available.

Activity

At the beginning of a lesson, present students with a verbal list of three to five questions. Review the questions to determine if students understand what is being asked. Then, switch on a tape (auditory or visual format) of a speaker and instruct students to listen for the answers to the questions in the speaker's lecture. The tape can be teacher made or commercially produced. The exercise is most effective if the students are familiar with the type of information (through prior knowledge) but it is not a topic they are currently studying in class (so that they do not immediately know the answers to the questions). Do not stop the tape or replay it for students. At the conclusion of the presentation, repeat the first question to students and ask them to write the answer on a sheet of paper. Repeat this until students have answered all the questions. (For an added challenge, add a question that cannot be answered by the information on the tape recording).

Begin by using only audio recordings since videotapes will give students visual cues to information. As students begin to develop better listening skills, include video presentations since that is a common method of information delivery outside the classroom. Increase the difficulty of questions from simply recall to application and analysis questions as students continue to improve their listening skills. Repeat this exercise on a weekly basis to continue working to develop students' listening skills, varying the type of information on the tape to include topics of interest to students. This will encourage them to listen more closely and, in doing so, hone their listening skills.

NOTE-TAKING STRATEGY #4

Background

One of the most effective ways to organize auditory material is to listen for a definite pattern in the words or phrases. A group of words strung together is easier to recall if an organizer such as alphabetical order is included. This strategy works in many listening games, such as this activity where students play a round-robin style game using alphabetical or numerical sequence. The alphabetical or numerical sequence makes this game ideal for primary grade students.

Activity

Select a category—in this example, it's grocery store shopping—then introduce the listening chain with a statement containing a word that fits the category and begins with the letter A: "I went to the grocery store and bought an apple." Call on a student to add their B purchase to your shopping list: "I went to the grocery store and bought an apple and some bananas." Select another student randomly to add another item to the list: "I went to the grocery store and bought an apple, some bananas, and a cupcake." Continue to call on students randomly, more than once if possible, to add another item to the list after successfully reciting all the earlier items. There is a twofold use for primary students: they have an opportunity to repeat the alphabet while listing the sequence of grocery store purchases. Continue the game until you reach item Z (zucchini?) or until the chain is broken when a student is unable to repeat the proper sequence of items. Try some of the categories listed below for primary students to improve listening skills.

Category Ideas

Animals	Clothing	Story Characters
Colors	Compound Words	Famous Places
First Names	Foods	Jobs
Emotions	School Supplies	Vehicles
Games	Action Words	Describing Words

NOTE-TAKING STRATEGY #5

Background

The Cornell Note-Taking System (Pauk, 2000) consists of multiple related tasks organized in a pattern to maximize long-term concept retention. Students can learn the technique in a few hours and teachers can incorporate it easily into existing classroom study programs. The system, sometimes known as the "Six Rs"—record, reduce, recall, recite, reflect, review—is designed to provide specific study strategies for a variety of alternate style learners.

Activity

Begin with an 8½ × 11-inch sheet of paper. Divide the paper into two columns. The left hand (recall) column should be approximately 2½ inches and the right hand (record) column should be approximately 6 inches. At the bottom of the paper, leave a 2-inch margin. Students can prepare the paper themselves or, at the onset of using this method, teachers can prepare sample sheets so that the students understand the layout and approximate proportions of the system.

When a lecturer begins speaking, students should take notes in phrases (not complete sentences) in the right hand (record) column. These notes should be brief, highlighting the essential key terms (students may want to write key terms in all capital letters for emphasis). After the lecture (ideally this should take place as soon as possible, directly following the lecture), students should reread the notes in the record column and "reduce" the concept or information there to a key term (one to two words). This term should be written in the left hand (recall) column.

To complete the final steps, students should return to the notes later that day (or that evening at home) and "recite" the key terms in the "recall" column, while covering the notes in the record column in order to test their retention of the newly acquired material. Students can do this independently or with a study buddy, and the process should be repeated for a few days so that students become comfortable with the material before they "reflect" on the material and write a brief summary in the 2-inch margin at the bottom of their note-taking page. Students should then continue to "review" their notes on a regular basis, even comparing them to a friend's notes for clarification. Developing a regular routine of note review will reduce anxiety in the hours before an examination since the material will already be familiar to students from earlier review sessions. The Cornell Note-Taking System can also be used as a study aid for exam preparation.

NOTE-TAKING STRATEGY #6

Background

Like any skill, note taking improves with time and practice. However, a number of quick and easy strategies can make even well organized notes a little better. The following strategies can be posted in the classroom or photocopied for students to tape to the inside of their notebooks. There should be a few blank lines for students to write some of their personal note-taking strategies.

It is most effective for students to focus on one or two of the following strategies at first, incorporating others as they feel comfortable with the initial techniques. They can then pick the ones that work best for them and refine them. They'll see a big change in their notes, while you may witness an even bigger improvement in their test scores.

Activity

Begin with a discussion of study techniques, and consider setting aside one or two class periods to ensure students have a grasp on the desired goals. During the discussion, ask students to share some of the hints they have found helpful in studying material they have acquired during lectures. Since there are a variety of learning styles in any classroom, students can learn from one another if their learning styles are similar.

Have a copy of the list below available for students to discuss during the period. Knowing *why* they are employing these techniques may make students less reluctant to use them in their daily or weekly study routines. Review each strategy and provide students with time to ask questions. Leave space on the list for student additions.

- *Title and date each lecture for future reference. It may be helpful in locating a previous lecture that contains relevant information.*
- *Look directly at the speaker. You may detect some cues in voice, and gestures may alert you that a certain piece of information is more important than others.*
- *Use double spacing when writing notes. In this way, you can make additions later as you acquire more information on the topic.*
- *Review your notes before and after each class to refresh your memory about the topic and develop any questions you may want answered.*
- *Use a colored marker or highlighter for main ideas only. Using this type of tool excessively reduces its effectiveness.*

- *Never abbreviate key terms or vocabulary words. Be sure you have the correct spelling, and ask the lecturer to spell it for you if necessary.*
- *Complete any reading assignments before the lecture so that you are able to take more meaningful notes, linking what you read to what you hear.*
- *Write questions you have in the margin while the lecture is in progress, and ask them at the conclusion, or before if invited to do so by the speaker.*
- *Write down all information the speaker writes on a board or overhead projector. If the speaker considers it important to write down, then you should, too!*

NOTE-TAKING STRATEGY #7

Background

While educators are aware that most students have a marked preference for expressing their ideas (visual, auditory, kinesthetic), this variation in preferences is also true for the method in which students acquire and process information. Some students learn best from listening to a step-by-step explanation of how a particular instrument works while others would prefer to see a demonstration. Others may be most interested in actually trying to use the instrument themselves.

These varied preferences can also appear for students taking notes from a lecture or presentation, so it is beneficial to have more than one note-taking strategy for these alternate style learners.

Activity

The concept of webbing and mapping is not unfamiliar to educators who have put it to use with prereading and prewriting exercises. But, you may not realize that these activities can be used effectively for note taking as well. In particular, concept mapping is a favorite among visual learners. It enables these students to see the entire picture at one time so that they can visualize the relationships that occur between the concepts.

Have students begin with a sheet of paper, turned either horizontally or vertically. Date the top of the paper (for future reference) and place a square or circle in the middle of the paper. Inside that shape, instruct students to write the topic of the lecture or presentation.

During the course of the lecture, instruct students to write some of the minor ideas outside the square or circle, using a thin line to connect them to the topic. If two or more of the minor ideas relate to one another, they should draw lines to illustrate that connection. Any supporting details should be placed around the idea they describe, with lines linking them to that idea. The completed concept map will bear a slight resemblance to a spider with a centrally located body and several appendages coming from that body.

NOTE-TAKING STRATEGY #8

Background

To help students develop better note-taking habits, the same emphasis should be placed on teaching these skills as a prereading or prewriting lesson. Linking new information to prior knowledge is a key note-taking strategy. It is important to stress to students that when they review their notes, they are organizing them to fit with what they already know about the topic. Students should also be encouraged to rework phrases from their notes into questions that they can ask themselves or their study buddy. Being able to manipulate the information into other formats gives students a firmer grasp of what they have learned.

Activity

Once students have been taking notes for some time, they are prepared to learn a few more techniques for making the most of what they have written during a lecture or presentation. Use some of the questions listed below to help students identify connections between what they have learned and what they already know about a topic. Teachers may also wish to add additional questions specific to a particular topic. Also, have students review their notes, then jot down a question that they would still like to have answered concerning the topic. Answer these questions during a class period so that students can make the necessary changes to their notes.

- *What are three key vocabulary terms and what does each word mean?*
- *List three ways that this information affects your daily life.*
- *What group of people (career, culture, age group) would benefit most from knowing this information?*
- *What inventions are possible today due to this information? What type of modern day conveniences might not be here today if this information had not been available?*
- *How does this new information relate to the knowledge you have already acquired regarding this topic?*
- *What place(s) could you visit to learn more about this topic?*
- *Why do you think this information is studied in your grade?*
- *Can you name one Web site that might provide more information about this topic?*
- *What else would you like to know about this topic? Why?*

NOTE-TAKING STRATEGY #9

Background

Taking notes from a lecture or presentation requires a certain set of skills. Some of these skills can also be useful for taking notes with reading assignments. Many students feel that taking notes from reading assignments is pointless because the information is already printed in the book. Rewriting, reworking, and reviewing this material, however, can help students increase chances for long-term retention. Introducing some of these methods to students, then, will help them make better use of their homework reading time.

Activity

Students in late middle school or high school often have multiple reading assignments in their classes. Therefore, it is a good idea to develop a uniform method of note-taking strategies for lectures as well as for homework reading assignments. An activity for the latter involves using Post-it Notes of various colors (many office supply stores sell multicolor packs). Have students begin by designating a color for each category in their notes. For example, when a vocabulary term is introduced, they should write the term and a brief definition on a yellow note, leaving it stuck to the page where it was introduced. If the reading contains a sequenced explanation (how a bill becomes a law; how a tornado occurs; how a cell is divided), they should write the term and the number of steps involved on a blue note. Key reference sources, such as Web sites or related reading, can be printed on a pink note. Instruct them to leave all of the notes adhered to the page on which the information was located. Remind them, also, to be sure to read an assignment *before* attending the lecture on that information, because the new information will have more meaning if key terms and concepts have already been introduced in the reading. After the lecture, individually or with a study buddy, students should reread the Post-it Notes, adding any information that relates to what is already on those slips of colored paper. The notes should be kept in place and used when it is time to review for an examination, as it will make locating the information much easier than a random scan of the entire chapter.

NOTE-TAKING STRATEGY #10

Background

Note-taking strategies, like most other skills taught in school, improve and develop with practice. Note taking tips should, therefore, be shared with students on a regular basis. Some of the tips listed below can be used to help students sharpen their note-taking strategies.

Activity

- *Use some form of color-coding with notes. For example, use blue index cards and a blue notebook for all American history notes; use green index cards and a green notebook for science notes. This will help save preparation time.*
- *Always complete the reading assignment before the lecture. The new information will have more meaning when it can be connected to the information that was acquired from the chapter(s).*
- *Date each lecture and write a topic heading. This will help in organizing the notes and locating them for preexamination review.*
- *Never abbreviate key vocabulary terms. Ask for correct spelling at the time of the lecture.*
- *Use an existing note-taking system (i.e., Cornell System) or develop one of your own that makes information accessible and easy to read and understand.*
- *Review notes on a regular basis, making additions as new information and explanations become available.*

CHAPTER SIX

Building and Reinforcing Student Vocabulary

One's vocabulary needs constant fertilizing or it will die.

—Evelyn Waugh

With the exception of individuals dealing with specific learning challenges, learners possess four distinct, yet overlapping, vocabularies—listening, speaking, reading, and writing. A listening vocabulary is the first to develop and grows even before a child learns to speak. It is from this listening vocabulary that a speaking vocabulary develops as very young children choose words that have meaning in their lives to initiate their first speech. Parents and guardians wait anxiously for a baby's "first word" and often place great emphasis on which word is the first one in a child's speaking vocabulary. While family debates may revolve around the issue of whether a child uttered "Mommy" or "Daddy," more often the choice is simply made based on which syllables the child finds least difficult to pronounce.

Most children begin to build a reading vocabulary (words they can recognize in print) before they begin formal education; those who haven't may find themselves at a disadvantage in groups with classmates who have been read to by parents and other family members long before the first school bell rings. As students begin to express themselves in print, their writing vocabulary emerges. At the onset, this vocabulary is smaller than the other three and often remains that way for some time. One of the primary goals of any literacy program should be to reduce the disparity that occurs between these four areas so that literate learners are able to comprehend what information is being conveyed, and subsequently formulate and express a verbal or written response.

A meaningful literacy program should contain a vocabulary component that provides learners with the opportunity to acquire words as they become necessary for daily life. For example, it is relatively pointless to introduce a student to a comprehensive list of –able and –ible words as they are presented in a conventional spelling textbook. Vocabulary acquisition is more meaningful when the words presented relate to one another and to the learner's daily routine, such as the name words of "desk," "chair," "pencil," and "paper" to a beginning kindergartener or the terms, "analyze," "dissect," and "hypothesize" for a middle school science student. Additionally, activities intended to reinforce new vocabulary should engage learners through the use of a high-interest approach such as a game or puzzle. Once underway, building and maintaining a solid vocabulary provides students with another important tool for gathering new information and expressing themselves to one another.

USING THIS CHAPTER

While some of the activities in this chapter are geared toward a particular type of word (synonym, compound word), many can be modified to use any sort of vocabulary list that is relevant for the situation. The primary emphasis in many of these vocabulary-building strategies is to help students identify and understand the relationship that exists between words. This can be achieved through a study of word origins or by grouping the words into categories based on definition or function.

The growing population of ESL learners requires developing different types of vocabulary exercises. Students of various ages need to receive basic instruction in the English language in order to comprehend written and verbal directions for completing daily assignments.

Some vocabulary activities provide reinforcement and practice in the form of games or worksheets, while other activities provide students with tools they will be able to use well beyond classroom walls to tackle new and unfamiliar words. Vocabulary acquisition is a lifelong pursuit and students must be equipped with strategies that will serve them throughout their lives.

There are a number of vocabulary exercises available on the Internet as well as in computer software packages. When deciding which of these programs is worthwhile, establish criteria that measure level of accessibility (look for user-friendly sites or software), practicality (examine options that will teach strategies students can use throughout their lives), and overall value (many online vocabulary are free; investigate these options before purchasing software that contains a finite set of words and activities).

VOCABULARY #1

Background

Word puzzles are a great way to get students excited about developing their vocabularies because these exercises are easy to understand and often rooted in humor. Even the most reluctant learner will find it difficult to resist the challenge of solving these puzzles before the rest of the class. Puzzles and riddles provide a painless way to reinforce vocabulary being presented through direct instruction.

Activity

Homophones are words that sound alike but have different meanings. Have students try to guess the homophone pairs in each phrase (examples below), either working alone or as a class. After students have completed enough of these riddles, challenge them to devise some of the own homophone pairs to share in class.

Homophone List

Riddle	Answer
rabbit fur	*hare hair*
sweet Bambi	*dear deer*
motionless writing paper	*stationary stationery*
an arrogant blood vessel	*vain vein*
undecorated aircraft	*plain plane*
the entire cavity	*whole hole*
tired vegetable	*beat beet*
assistance for an assistant	*aide aid*
dessert for caribou	*moose mousse*
60 minutes we spend together	*our hour*
window glass discomfort	*pane pain*
letters for boys and men	*male mail*
to encounter pepperoni	*meet meat*
a sailor's belly button	*naval navel*
advice from a panel of experts	*council counsel*
the story of a dog's wagger	*tail tale*

baby antelope	*new gnu*
naked cub	*bare bear*
go ahead and stitch	*so sew*
constructed by the housekeeper	*maid made*
to view a large body of water	*see sea*
cornflakes continuing story	*cereal serial*
smart money	*cents sense*
a stallion with a sore throat	*hoarse horse*
a just fee	*fair fare*
bargain event on boating equipment	*sail sale*
an amazing stunt at the end of your legs	*feet feat*
a wobbly seven days	*weak week*
fee levied on hardware equipment	*tacks tax*

VOCABULARY #2

Background

A card game already familiar to many students is an excellent foundation for constructing new vocabulary development activities. The games can focus on any one aspect of language such as compound words, prefixes, or suffixes and can be built around the rules of hearts, gin rummy, go fish, or old maid. For an added challenge, have students work in groups (three to four students) to create the decks themselves. After writing the words on one side, they can draw the same picture on the back of every card in the deck, thus creating a realistic looking deck. At the end of the school year, raffle off the decks and repeat the process with a new group of students the next year.

Activity

Two to four students can play this variation of gin rummy that involves synonyms and antonyms. Have students create a deck in multiples of three, using a pattern that offers a word and one synonym and antonym for that word. For example, write a card for the word "large," for its synonym, "big," and for its antonym, "small." Other examples include "over-above-below," "huge-gigantic-tiny," and "complete-entire-partial." The completed deck should have at least thirty-six to thirty-nine cards (twelve or thirteen synonym/antonym triads).

The dealer should deal each player five cards, then place the remaining cards in the middle of the table. Players then draw and discard as they attempt to make synonym pairs (worth one point per pair) or antonym pairs (worth two points per pair) with their cards. Players wishing to take a card from the discard pile that is not on top of the stack must also collect any cards discarded after the desired card. Since synonym pairs are worth fewer points than antonym pairs, players may want to wait until they can make an antonym pair. However, since only the winner's points are tallied, players may want to use up the cards they are holding on any available pair. Play should continue until one player reaches twenty-five points. As in rummy, players can lay down an antonym to go with another player's synonym pair or vice versa. You may also want to consider laminating these cards so that they can be used throughout the school year.

VOCABULARY #3

Background

Many high school students tend to glide over unfamiliar words when reading a science or social studies text, assuming that they have enough information from the other words to construct meaning from the passage. Unfortunately, there are times when the less familiar word is a key factor in comprehending the material. By scanning over the word without attempting to determine its meaning from context cues or by using a dictionary, readers lose a critical component that diminishes their grasp of the information. Identifying ways to make students slow down (or stop) on these new and unfamiliar words provides an opportunity to offer some indirect instruction, such as the cloze method sometimes used to determine a student's ability to read and comprehend a written passage. (Every seventh or ninth word is removed from a written passage to determine if students can comprehend the text at a sufficient level to fill in the missing words.)

Activity

This activity can be completed using a written passage from a newspaper or news magazine, the Internet, or from a student science or social studies text. Reprint a section of text from one of those sources, removing every seventh or ninth word similar to the cloze method. Be sure not remove key vocabulary terms or proper names, and avoid removing connector words such as "the," "and," or "but." Replace the deleted word with a blank line, aiming for ten to twelve blank words in a three-paragraph passage. At the bottom of the passage, compile a word bank of the deleted words adding three to five more words so that students are unable to complete the assignment using process of elimination of terms. After the worksheet has been completed, use some of the questions listed below in a discussion or as part of an informal journal entry.

- *How many of the blanks were you able to fill without any difficulty?*
- *Name two blank spaces that presented problems for you, and explain how you determined which words fit into those spaces.*
- *Name one of the blank spaces from the passage and substitute the word you placed there with its synonym. Does the passage still make sense?*
- *What made you decide not to use some of the terms in the word bank?*
- *Replace the first blank space with the word's antonym, and explain how the new word changes the meaning of the passage.*

VOCABULARY #4

Background

Student-created decks of word play cards accomplish a number of classroom objectives. They provide a highly stimulating drill practice for various language concepts, and because the students actually create the cards themselves, the process involves students in multiple steps in the learning process. Creating room supplies like this also gives students a sense of ownership and investment in the learning community, making these items and the use of them much more appealing and motivating to students during independent activities.

Activity

Have students create a deck of compound words, separating each word onto two cards. For example, the compound word, "railroad," would be divided with "rail" written on one card and "road" written on another card. Students may work in small groups (three to four members) to brainstorm a list of compound words before creating the decks.

To play the game, place students in groups of no more than six players and make sure each deck contains no fewer than thirty pairs of compound words. Instruct each group to appoint a dealer who will distribute five cards to each player before placing the next card face up in the center of the playing surface. Players, in turn, draw and discard one card, attempting to form compound words that they will display face up before them. As in traditional rummy, they may choose to use the face-up card on the discard pile instead of drawing from the deck. Players wishing to use a card on the discard pile that is not the top card must also collect any cards discarded after the desired card. Play should continue until one player uses all of his or her cards to form compound words, determining the winner who receives fifteen points. If no player can accomplish this by the time the final card is drawn, the player with the most compound words wins that round of play and is awarded a score of ten points. To add an informal evaluation to the activity, ask each student provide a brief definition of the compound word (to be checked in a dictionary) to receive one point per definition.

VOCABULARY #5

Background

Games are among the most useful tools in vocabulary development and reinforcement because they can be constructed and adapted for virtually every unit of study. The rules remain the same, but the content of each set of cards or game board can be suited to a specific subject area. These activities provide excellent drill practice in science and social studies classes, and provide a lively method of test review. An extra dimension is added to the exercise when students are involved in the actual construction of the games.

Activity

Create this game with blank (no numbers) bingo cards and any five-letter word. Distribute the cards, computer-generated or student creations, and then announce a five-letter word that students should print across the top of the card. For example, have students write the word, S-T-A-C-K.

Next, designate a category for each horizontal row and have students write words from that category that begin with the letter listed at the top of the column. For example, if the first category is "animals," they might complete the middle row "A" of their STACK card with the words, "snake," "tiger," "ape," "cat," and "kangaroo." Repeat this process with four more categories for each card. (As in traditional bingo, it is not necessary to leave a blank space in the center of the card.) Students proceed to fill all twenty-five spaces with appropriate words.

Once the spaces are filled, begin calling on students to volunteer the words they listed for each of the five categories. If other students in the room share the same word (for example, if three other students have the word, "snake"), the student reading the list and the students who have the same word must cover that space on their card. Continue the game with students sharing words from their cards and classmates with corresponding responses covering those spaces or words on their STACK cards.

The object of STACK is to think of words for each category that are less common, so that there is less likelihood that other students will have the same word on their cards. When all students have shared each of their responses, the winner is the student(s) who has a straight line, diagonal, or four corners still uncovered (meaning no one else had that word). If no one has one of these configurations, the winner is the student with the most uncovered spaces on a card. As a follow-up, discuss with students which categories and/or letters were the most difficult to complete. For an added challenge, have winners give a brief definition of the words left uncovered.

VOCABULARY #6

Background

One of the many benefits of using games in the classroom is that students have an opportunity to interact with one another beyond just lunchtime and recess, allowing for a different form of communication with peers. For example, when students work in groups to construct the games, they are developing valuable cooperative learning skills. The actual game-playing process fosters fair play and good sportsmanship as well as an understanding of winning and losing graciously.

Activity

Have students create a deck of compound words, or start with the deck created in Vocabulary Activity #4, separating each word onto two cards. For example, with the word, "lifestyle," "life" would appear on one card while "style" would appear on a second card. Make sure each deck contains no fewer than thirty pairs of compound words plus one blank card for each student in the class. With students in groups of three to four, have one student deal each person seven word cards and one blank card. Next, turn up one card to begin the word chain. If the first player cannot add to the beginning or end of that card to form a compound word, the player must draw a card from the deck. Players may also choose to use their blank card as a wild card to supply a response, but caution them that using the card too early in the game may reduce their options for play later.

The game should continue as players either add onto the existing chain or draw a card from the deck. Players do not have to lay a card down for each draw but they must draw a card or use one from their existing hand. The word chain continues until one player uses all of his or her cards. Sample word chains are "day-light-house-boat-man" or "waste-basket-ball-room-mate." For an added challenge, students may begin building chains from cards discarded and used earlier in the game. For example, if the word chain contains the words, "day-light-house-boat," a player with nothing to add to "boat" can attempt to add to the chain horizontally by adding something to one of the earlier words, placing the new card beside the word chain, such as "bird" placed to the left of "house," or "time" added to the right of "day."

VOCABULARY #7

Background

Activities that allow students to move around the room help them release some of the energy that builds up after a morning or afternoon of seatwork. Such activities provide a productive outlet that can replace trips to the pencil sharpener several times a day. These activities work particularly well for kinesthetic learners—students who function best when engaged in some kind of physical movement.

Activity

Working as a class, create a list of compound words. A good number is at least twice as many words as students in the class so students can find lots of matches. Then, have students construct a deck of cards containing the compound words, separating each word onto two cards; for example, "wallpaper" would appear on two cards as "wall" and "paper." Encourage students to write on the cards in large, easily visible letters.

Have each student select one card—half of a compound word—from the deck lying face down on a table. Then, give students five to ten minutes to circulate among classmates to find any words that, when combined with their card, form a compound word. The word can be connected to the front or back of the word (the level of nonproductive noise will indicate when students have completed this portion of the activity). Next, instruct them to divide the other side of their card into two columns. In the left hand column, tell students to write down the words they made up using word parts from other classmates. Once these are recorded, ask them to return to their seats and to try and think of more compound words using the "half" word printed on their card. A specific number of words (three to four) can be set or students can be challenged to write as many as possible. These new words should then be written on the right hand column of the card.

In a postactivity discussion, have students share their words with classmates using some of these questions.

- *How did the placement of your word (beginning or end of new compound word) affect its meaning?*
- *Does your word seem to have more words successfully attached to its beginning, or to its end, to form compound words? Why do you think that is true?*
- *How much of the meaning of the original two words is retained when they form a compound word? Explain your response and give at least two examples.*

VOCABULARY #8

Background

Word webs can be effective tools for determining how much prior knowledge students have about certain words. They are particularly useful at the beginning of a unit of study where assessing student background knowledge directs the course of instruction.

Activity

Begin by writing a vocabulary word in the center of the web, and surround the word with a number of questions or statements. Have students work independently or in small groups to respond to the questions. In the case of small group brainstorming with word webs, pool the results of each group's findings to create a projected profile of classroom prior knowledge.

Once the word webs are filled in with student responses, words may be classified in a number of ways. The webbing questions and statements help determine students' understanding of nouns, verbs, and adjectives. Similar web exercises could deal with affixes, definitions, and other parts of speech.

Sample questions for noun, verb, and adjective webs are listed below.

Noun

- *How would you make a _____?*
- *Where could you find a _____?*
- *When should you use a _____?*
- *Why would you want/need a _____?*

Verb

- *Who knows how to _____?*
- *In what locations can you _____?*
- *What do you need in order to _____?*
- *Why do people want/need to _____?*

Adjective

- *Name three things that are _____.*
- *Describe ways to avoid being _____.*
- *List ways to become/feel _____.*
- *List words that mean the same as _____.*

VOCABULARY #9

Background

For ESL students, one of the more difficult language forms to comprehend is the *idiom*. Unfortunately, this is one of the most common word forms they will encounter on an average day. These students often feel more isolated from their peers due, in part, to the fact that while they are learning English, they are confused about the construction of idioms and often make an inappropriate substitution, such as a "Danny horse" in the leg after a strenuous exercise session. While many English-speaking students do not know the origin of every idiom they use, they are aware that a specific name, "Charlie," correctly completes the idiom listed before.

Activity

Visit Internet sites, such as www.idiomsite.com, that feature lists of idioms along with their origins. Encourage students to collect more idioms from their family and friends to share with the class, and compile a list to post in the classroom. Next, place students into pairs, giving each pair a separate idiom. Challenge the students to find out more about the idiom and how it came into existence, as well as to what topic it relates (sports, medicine, music). For example, when someone presents an idea that is so far removed from the topic being discussed that its inclusion is almost laughable, such an idea is often referred to as "out in left field," which refers to that far-off position on a baseball diamond.

Once the students have located information about the idiom, instruct them to find a creative way to present it to the rest of the class. Students may wish to use illustrations or creative dramatics to share their findings with the rest of the class, and for further review, there are examples of children's literature, such as Fred Gwynne's *A Little Pigeon Toad*, that celebrate the humor of idioms. For an added challenge, have students make up their own idioms using the same strategies involved in existing idioms. Share these creations with the rest of the class or on a classroom or hallway bulletin board.

VOCABULARY #10

Background

Recognizing the categories in which words fit such as *describer,* *action, naming,* or so on requires a solid understanding of the word's meaning, including its multiple definitions. The word "seed," for example, has a number of definitions. While "seed" would fit appropriately into a discussion of farming, it would also fit into a discussion of team or player ranking in sports.

Students are often confused about how to classify multiple-definition words. An exercise that asks students to examine a word's various functions allows teachers to see the thought processes students use to classify vocabulary.

Activity

Place students in small groups (three to four members) and provide each group with eighteen to twenty-five index cards, each containing a word from texts used in class or from student writing (this number may vary based on the group's grade or ability level). Groups should also be given a transparency sheet and an overhead marker. Ask each group to sort the words into categories, creating the category headings through group discussion. For example, they might group the words, "playful," "beach," and "hotel" under the heading of "vacation." Tell them to avoid labels that reflect no read understanding of the word, such as "number of letters" or "syllables." Remind them, also, to examine the words for their relationship to one another as well as their function and/or meaning. Each category must have at least two words and words may appear in only one category.

Next, ask students to write the list of category headings on the transparency sheet with the words listed in their appropriate categories. Appoint a group spokesperson to share the lists with classmates.

Students with a more tenuous grasp of the word's meaning will stick with simple headings such as "descriptive words" or "action words" while students who have a clear idea of the word's meaning can place it under a more complex heading such as "feelings people have" or "objects that are used as tools."

This activity works equally well if all groups have the same set of words or if each group has a different set. To avoid one group member monopolizing the creation of categories, tell the groups that each student must create at least one category.

VOCABULARY #11

Background

One of the best indicators of student vocabulary levels is an ability to supply more descriptive synonyms in written composition. Instead of trying to describe a house as "very very big," students with a more developed vocabulary might choose words like "spacious" or "immense" that give readers a clearer view of the structure's size and stature. Examples of these more complex synonyms can be found in students' texts as well as fiction and nonfiction books in the classroom or school library. Use the examples below and the subsequent questions in the activity section as the basis for a discussion about using synonyms.

- *What is a simple word that means the same as the larger word?*
- *Which word provides a better image of what the author is describing? What make you say that?*
- *Give two reasons for choosing to use the larger or more descriptive word even though both words have the same basic definition.*

Activity

For this exercise, present students with a list of twenty to twenty-five words or short phrases. Challenge students to identify at least two more complex or descriptive synonyms for each of the terms on the list. For example, the phrase, "moved slowly" might offer a more vivid picture with the verb "lumbered." Vary the selections, listing simple nouns, verbs, and adjectives that can benefit from the substitution of a more complex synonymous term. For a variation of this exercise, present students with a set of images of buildings or of living beings (people, animals) engaged in all sorts of activities. For the buildings, instruct students to write a vivid description of the structure, focusing on size, shape or physical condition of the building. For the living beings, challenge students to write a description of what type of activity the characters are currently engaged in with the most vivid verbs possible. ("The squirrel *scampered* up the tree:" The bridesmaids *chattered* excitedly and *gushed* at the sight of the bride when she appeared in the doorway.") Some of the images and accompanying statements can then be posted on a bulletin board as a reminder to use the most expressive terms when writing compositions.

VOCABULARY #12

Background

One type of connection between two words or phrases is referred to as an *analogous* relationship. For example, an analogy linking gloves and hats can be made by stating that "a glove is to a hand as a hat is to a head," demonstrating that while a glove covers a hand, the corresponding part of the body that is covered by a hat is the head. An ability to draw analogies between words and word pairs indicates that a reader has a solid grasp of word meaning and usage. If, for example, a student using the analogy listed above states "a glove is to a hand as a hat is to a scarf" or "a glove is to a hand as a hat is to a foot," the student does not have a clear idea of the relationship between a glove and hand and cannot, therefore, replicate it in the second half of the analogical statement. This connection calls for a more complex thought process and can be used to help students build and reinforce vocabulary.

Activity

Ordinarily, analogy statements contain four elements. The first two elements relate to one another; the second two statements relate to one another and are comparable to the first pair. To hone in on these elements, compile a list of several analogy statements, and present students with this list that omits one element from each statement. For example, from the analogy listed above, alter the statement to read, "glove is to hand as hat is to _____" or "glove is to hand as _____ is to head" challenging students to complete the analogy with an appropriate word. The analogies can be related to a unit currently being studied, or can be taken from student writing or reading passages. Listed below are some examples of analogy pairs.

- *Simple is to complex as small is to large. (antonyms)*
- *Shiny is to glistening as big is to enormous. (synonyms)*
- *Glasses are to eyes as hearing aid is to ears. (medical device)*
- *Luxurious is to lavish as rustic is to bucolic. (synonyms)*
- *Mozart is to music as Renoir is to art. (masters of an art)*
- *House is to room as hour is to minute. (contained within)*

After completing the activity, use the questions below to guide a postactivity discussion.

- *What is the first relationship you examined in the phrase? Why?*
- *How does the first pair of words relate to the second pair?*
- *What would happen if you removed more than one word from the analogy statement?*
- *Provide the first half of an analogy statement on a sheet of paper. Hand the paper to a classmate who will attempt to complete the analogy statement.*

VOCABULARY #13

Background

Presenting vocabulary in a way that enhances readers' likelihood of retention should be a primary goal for any language program. Unfortunately, the methods in which vocabulary are presented in many spelling and English grammar texts often fail to capitalize on that aspect on instruction. Instead, words tend to be grouped by affixes, number of syllables, and other less meaningful categories. Consequently, students do not learn the words' relationship to one another or to daily living. Exercises rooted in these two principles tend to result in higher levels of long-term retention by readers.

Activity

Young, less experienced readers tend to believe that there is one word for everything in their language and that word can be used in all situations. For example, the word, "laugh," should be used whenever a character has a humorous reaction to what another character has said or done. The word, however, represents only one aspect of this behavior. Story characters can guffaw, chuckle, snicker, giggle, or chortle depending on their mood and personality. Introducing students to the entire world of laughter gives them an opportunity to give a more precise term in their own writing. Jolly old St. Nick may prefer to "chuckle" at a funny story while the members of the babysitters' club may "giggle" at the same story.

Begin this activity by selecting a concept. It can be an action word (verb), describing word (adjective or adverb) or a naming word (noun). Present a number of words that have a similar meaning (such as "guffaw," "chuckle," or "chortle") to students along with their definitions. Then read a definition and challenge students (individually or in pairs) to actively demonstrate an action (verb), or draw an image (noun or adjective). Initially, allow students to take turns in an informal activity to become accustomed to the subtle nuances that exist between the vocabulary words. Next, develop an activity for the words that challenge students to think about how to demonstrate the most precise meaning of the word. Be sure, while doing so, that students are familiar with one half of the equation, such as animals or people so that they can impose the less familiar vocabulary terms with greater ease. A sample activity might have the students reflect on the many terms associated with humorous reaction by naming which animal might guffaw, giggle, chortle, chuckle, or snicker based on the animal's size, characteristics, and proposed behaviors. (Bears are too large to giggle while long, squirmy lemurs might feel right at home snickering to one another.) As an extension to this activity, students can illustrate or dramatize the animals' unique humorous reactions.

VOCABULARY #14

Background

Many of today's teachers were educated in a school system where vocabulary was introduced and reinforced by having students look up and write the vocabulary term and its accompanying definition. Experience has proven this method to be less than effective in terms of long-term retention or increased usage of the new words. If students' exposure to such words as "tremendous," "titanic," or "colossal" is restricted to a nonrelated vocabulary exercise, they are likely to continue calling the Milky Way a "really big place" where the earth is located. The key to a meaningful vocabulary activity, then, lies in identifying a way to encourage students to look beyond the printed definition of a word to its use in everyday life.

Activity

To develop an activity stressing the definition of adjectives or adverbs, introduce the words to students during an informal small or large group discussion, using examples found in their daily reading from textbooks, or stories, and magazines. Talk about how the word can be used in place of a more familiar word, for example, "gigantic" can be used to emphasize the size of a "really big" object, giving the reader a clearer mental image. Next, compose a list of statements or questions that include the word for students to answer. An appropriate response will demonstrate a deep understanding of the vocabulary term, while an inappropriate response will help teachers pinpoint the origin of a student's confusion. Here are some sample statements and questions to use as a guideline in developing this type of activity.

- *Identify three "luxurious" fabrics, and include your reason for those choices.*
- *What four purchases might an "impulsive" shopper make? What makes you say that?*
- *What events might call for an "exuberant" response? What makes you say that?*
- *Would a "loquacious" or "laconic" person make a better keynote speaker for an event? Why do think that is so?*
- *Name three occasions when treading "gingerly" might be considered a good idea? What makes you say that?*

VOCABULARY #15

Background

Alternate style learners and ESL students often struggle with written expression even when they know the correct response. Including alternate methods of assessment can give these students an opportunity to demonstrate their knowledge as well as experience success in the classroom. Vocabulary exercises are a great way to get these students actively involved in the learning process by allowing them to share what they know in a less conventional method.

Activity

Many kinesthetic learners invest time and energy in seeking ways to be out of their seats. Developing a vocabulary activity that satisfies that desire will often yield greater participation from these students. Find a group of related action words (verbs) to introduce to the class in small or large groups, and discuss the words, focusing upon how they are the same and different from one another. (Walking and lumbering are both locomotive activities but differ in execution.) Then, identify examples of the words in student reading and clarify their meanings in informal discussions. After the students have worked with the words for a specified period of time, use an alternate method of assessment to monitor their grasp of the definitions. The words can then be written on separate index cards and one card presented to each student. Challenge students to present their words to the rest of the class in a charade-like format using gestures and other nonverbal cues to share their own understanding of the word with classmates. As they present, allow the class to make guesses about which word is being demonstrated. As an added activity, students can be divided into teams and each team can be responsible for presenting a certain number of words. For visual spatial learners, an opportunity to draw what some of the new naming words (nouns) they have learned look like may provide far more detailed responses than a simple regurgitation of the dictionary definition. These illustrations can then be displayed on a classroom bulletin board to allow all the students to see a visual representation of the new vocabulary words.

CHAPTER SEVEN

Exploring Research Resources

A little knowledge that acts is worth infinitely more than much knowledge that is idle.

—Kahil Gibran

Using reference materials effectively requires the development of different skills than those used to read fiction or expository text. Since the primary purpose of reference texts is information gathering, students should be provided with opportunities that allow them to learn and perfect various methods of identifying and extracting data from a large variety of sources.

Increased reliance on Web sites as a research resource presents teachers with the challenge of developing mini-units to teach students how to make the most of Internet information. These lessons should include not only how to acquire information from the Web but how to identify the difference between fact-based sites and personal opinion blogs—the role each one plays in presenting information (Richardson, 2006).

Since students' Internet-related skills may differ greatly due to computer availability and personal interest, it is a wise use of time to determine beforehand how much (or little) students know about how to navigate an information superhighway that expands on an almost hourly basis. Teachers might also find it worth investing some time outside the classroom to increase their own Internet skills so that they can act as a competent facilitator for their students.

While a working knowledge of the Internet is essential for students in our increasingly technical society, attention must still be paid to other information sources. Teaching students to work with maps, directories, and encyclopedias gives them a more complete tool kit for conducting research in and beyond the classroom. Despite a slow and steady evolution away from printed research materials, this format will continue to exist in some form for a number of years. For this reason, students need exposure to how these resources are organized and used for information acquisition. Many students may be adept at finding directions to a destination using such Internet software as Mapquest, but cannot identify the capital city of a state or country from a classroom globe or road map. This gap in practical knowledge may not seem relevant until a high school student with a new driver's license finds himself or herself unable to use a road map to return to a main highway after taking an accidental detour from a proposed route.

With all sources—Internet, print, or nonprint—developing activities that enable students to extract information independently and analyze the relevance, rather than depend on prepackaged data that may contain strong author bias, should remain a primary goal for teachers of all grade levels.

USING THIS CHAPTER

The activities in this chapter can be used effectively as part of a mini-unit to introduce a particular resource, such as an atlas or an encyclopedia, or it can be part of a larger unit that requires students to make use of sources to obtain information. The first edition of this book was published in 1998, so in this second edition there is an increased Internet presence. Rather than referring to specific sites, however, which could be dismantled without notice, the Internet activities are more global in scope giving students tips for more effective ways to use the Internet to locate the most information in the least amount of time.

Students in primary grades need solid introductions to many reference sources that they will be using during the course of their formal education. Students in middle school and high school require more specific tips for getting the most from time spent online. The activities for students in these grade levels will be geared toward using the Internet and other references resources in connection with content area subject projects. Additionally, this chapter contains activities for ESL students who may need assistance in using everyday items such as telephone directories and street maps.

Assessment for these activities may be completed independently or as part of an overall evaluation reflecting effective student use of reference sources.

EXPLORING RESEARCH RESOURCE #1

Background

Dictionary

To become proficient in using reference materials, students must first know how to use the tools within these resources to assist them in their information-gathering efforts. The most effective way to introduce these tools, such as dictionary guide words or tables of contents, is to identify each item and use it in material students already know and understand. Building on prior knowledge and learning is key in creating a solid foundation for the newly acquired skill.

Activity

Assign ten students to print their surnames on pieces of pasteboard. Randomly select two of these students to act as *guide words*. Guide words are the pair of words that appear at the top of a dictionary page indicating that all words on that page are contained, in alphabetical order, between these two words. (Try to select two students for guide words whose surnames are far enough apart to accommodate other students fitting between the word pair). Have each of the remaining eight students take turns standing between the two guide words students, asking the class to tell whether or not the student's surname belongs on that dictionary page.

Assign a new group of ten students to print any noun, verb, adjective or other part of speech on a piece of pasteboard. Again, randomly select two of these students to act as the guide words. Challenge the class to state which of these two students should stand on the left to represent the first guide word on the page (alphabetically). Repeat the process with the eight remaining students standing between the student guide words to see if their word fits between the pair. Finally, assign a third group of ten students, instructing them to write a word beginning with a predetermined letter on the pasteboard. (For example, have all students write a word beginning with the letter "t.") Repeat the process once more, having each of the remaining eight students stand between the guide word representatives so that the class can determine if their word fits on that page. This final step simulates how real dictionary guide words would look on a dictionary page. In order to move students to that point, however, the activity differed by beginning with a word (the surname) that the student would know and understand.

After the third group has completed its task, challenge students at their desks to arrange the words (that the ten students are holding) into proper alphabetical order. For an added challenge, instruct students to think of a word that fits between word cards being held by Student #1 and Student #2; between Student #2 and Student #3, etc.

EXPLORING RESEARCH RESOURCE #2

Background

Newspaper

When mature readers encounter an unfamiliar term in their reading, they try to determine its meaning based on context. In a variation of this practice, if the unfamiliar word is removed, readers should have sufficient comprehension of the sentence that they are able to substitute a word to complete it. For example, in the sentence, "The sinister-looking caretaker left behind a *cryptic* message that left guests who made the unsettling discovery feeling somewhat uneasy." While readers may not be familiar with the word, "cryptic," they can use clues from the rest of the sentence to determine that cryptic may mean that the message was mysterious or unfamiliar in nature.

The words "sinister" or "unsettling" hint that things are not as they should be or that the message was not readily understood. Therefore, the message caused concern since it was left behind by a sinister-looking individual. If the word "cryptic" is omitted from the passage, students might substitute "mysterious" and still maintain the meaning of the sentence.

Activity

Distribute copies of a news story, either from a hard copy newspaper or an online source, blotting out every seventh or eighth word. The story can be popular culture or current events, or relate to something students are currently studying in class. (Teachers may decide to recopy the story, leaving a blank space in place of every seventh or eighth word.) Avoid blotting out proper names or titles. Instruct students to read the passage, then reread it, filling in the blank spaces with words they think would make sense in the passage. Next, distribute copies of the original article or display it on an overhead projector. Use some of the questions listed below to guide a discussion about the students' word choices.

- *What effect does the word(s) you substituted have on the meaning of the sentence or passage?*
- *What term is used to describe the words you used as substitutes?*
- *What other words in the sentences did you use to decide on an appropriate substitute word? Explain how you arrived at your word choice.*
- *What do you think influenced the author's word choice in the article?*
- *How helpful were words, like "the," "an" or endings like "ing" or "ed" in nearby words in helping you determine a substitution?*

If formal evaluation is desired, list the student word substitution and calculate a score based on the number of appropriate substitutions in relation to the total number of words substituted. ("Student made a total of eight appropriate substitutions out of a total of twenty blank spaces.")

EXPLORING RESEARCH RESOURCE #3

Background

Internet

Before the Internet became such an indispensable classroom resource, students compiling research for a term paper faced the challenge of sifting through hardcover volumes of encyclopedia sets, magazine articles, and newspapers to find enough reference information to develop a decent reference list. This process meant a huge investment of time for students with somewhat limited results. Fortunately, there are newer tools in use on the Web today to bring information right to classroom desktops. Learning how to use these tools means that students can concentrate more on actually writing the term paper than on burrowing through mountains of reference sources to find two or three useable chunks of information.

Activity

As Internet use in the classroom increases, teachers and students are discovering new tools to make research much easier and more accessible. One such tool is RSS (Rich Site Summary), which sorts through piles of net content in search of previously specified topics that are then delivered to the user's computer using a collector known as an aggregator. So, instead of wading through site after site, RSS patrons simply submit a set of preferences and are notified periodically as the aggregator collects and delivers the information to the desktop.

At the onset of a term paper assignment, familiarize students with how RSS and aggregators work and how these tools can help them use their research time more effectively. The first step is setting up an aggregator to collect your RSS feeds. While there are many newsreaders, one worth checking out is Bloglines.com for the simple reason that you can access your collected feed from anywhere you have an Internet connection. Have students take turns setting up an aggregator for their topic. The process is a relatively simply-, step-by-step sign-up system similar to the kind found on most subscription services. Once students have set up the aggregator, ask them to revisit it at least three times during that week to see what feed it has collected and sent to them via the RSS. If this is the first time students have used this method, remind them to read over some of the content to determine which of the feed will be most helpful to them in writing their term paper.

For an initial RSS assignment, have students write a brief article on their selected topic including seven to ten pieces of information they discovered using their aggregator. The article should also contain some mention of which types of sites seemed to contain the most useful information. For example, sites created by other students and collected by the aggregator might contain useful information, but a commercial site such as CNN.com might be better equipped to deliver a more comprehensive profile on the student's topic.

In the article, have students discuss the effect their keywords or key phrases had on how the information was gathered. For example, if the keyword, "pets," was used, the amount and variety of information might be more daunting than if students narrowed the information search by using the key phrase "pet assisted therapy" and received only feed that related directly to that specific field. Learning to work with these Internet tools provides a solid foundation for students who are preparing to enter a more tech-savvy society.

EXPLORING RESEARCH RESOURCE #4

Background

Dictionary

Many students have gotten into the practice of leafing aimlessly through a dictionary in search of a certain word. While they may understand the concept of alphabetical order, they experience some confusion about how the words within a single letter are arranged.

Activities that ask students to manipulate guide words take two forms: they require students to classify words by stating between which set of guide words they appear, or they require them to generate lists of words that might appear between any two designated guide words. Using both methods allows students to view the process from two perspectives. This is particularly an ideal arrangement for alternate style learners.

Activity

Divide the class into two teams, asking each team to supply one word with the same initial letter ("sack"-"sultry"). To earn a point, each team must supply a word that fits between those guide words ("sack"-"sat"-"seem"-"sultry"). Next, eliminate the two original guide words using the new words in their place. Repeat the process, challenging teams to identify new words that fit between the constantly shrinking set of guide words. The game should continue until one team is unable to supply a word to fit between the guide words.

This game can also be played in an alternate way: each student is given a card on which they write a word (all "s" words, all "t" words). Team #1 provides one half of the guide word pair while Team #2 provides the other half. The game commences in the same way with students submitting the words previously printed on the cards to form new guide words. Each team should also have one to two blank cards on which they may print a word once they have exhausted all of their preprinted words. Again, the game ends after one team cannot supply a useable word. The other team must supply one more word in order to be declared winner.

EXPLORING RESEARCH RESOURCE #5

Background

Telephone Directory

Teaching students how to use the telephone directory involves familiarizing them with its format (alphabetical order, guide words, subject classification, etc.) through activities that illustrate the impact of this reference guide on their daily lives. This practice is particularly useful for primary students and ESL students who are learning how to make use of English reference resources that are used every day.

Locating a best friend's name, address, and telephone number is often the only exposure some students have to this resource. So, allowing students to acquaint themselves with this book regularly can eliminate constantly calling directory assistance operators who place a charge on the user's phone number for each assistance call. This life skill will serve students far beyond their years in the classroom.

Activity

Give students, working independently or in pairs, a copy of a recent telephone directory. Some telephone companies will provide these to schools for educational purposes. If not, have students bring an extra copy from their home for use during this assignment. Distribute a worksheet and instruct students to complete as many questions as possible using the phone directory. Some sample questions are provided below, and others can be added to the list to meet individual needs.

- *On what page of the book does your phone number appear?*
- *What are the guide words for that page?*
- *How many other people share your surname?*
- *How many, if any, spelling variations of your surname are in the book? What are the other spellings?*
- *List three streets that share your zip code.*
- *Name the grocery store nearest our school.*
- *How many florists are listed in this directory?*
- *List three headings under which you could find stores that sell computers.*
- *Locate a large ad—at least one fourth of the page—for a restaurant and list five facts contained in the advertisement.*
- *What communities does this phone directory serve?*

- *Identify an ad that contains more than one language. If you recognize the other language, can you name it?*
- *On what page does the listing for our school appear?*
- *How many separate numbers are listed for our school? Name two of the departments that have separate numbers.*
- *Into how many sections is this directory divided? Name the sections.*
- *How are names arranged in the telephone directory?*
- *How can you determine which businesses accept credit cards?*
- *Locate an ad for a store or restaurant you like to visit. Name four facts contained in the advertisement.*

EXPLORING RESEARCH RESOURCE #6

Background

Telephone Directory

Putting proper names in correct sequence employs different rules than conventional alphabetizing. Attention is given first to initials versus full names, apostrophes and ampersands are considered, and numbers are also added to the mix.

The best place to look for such examples is in the commerce section of the telephone directory. In this section, where businesses are listed in a category apart from private residences, students can analyze the rules of another ordering system.

Activity

Have students select a particular business, for example, "furnace and air conditioning repair" or "women's apparel" that has at least ten entries. Instruct students to write each of these entries, listing the full name of the merchant, on a separate index card. Next, ask students to switch decks of index cards with a classmate sitting near them. Give students three to four minutes to arrange their pile of cards in the proper sequence before they confirm their work with the telephone directory. In a postactivity discussion, students can respond to the questions below.

- *Why did you choose to place the cards in this order?*
- *How did you deal with entries that began with initials, such as A-Abel Furnace/Air Conditioning Repair?*
- *How is the commerce section of the phone directory different from the residential section? Why do you think this is true?*
- *Name three ways in which the commercial and residential sections of the phone directory are alike?*

Use telephone directories from a metropolitan area, rather than a small village or township, to ensure a sufficient quantity of business listings. A great place to get discarded phone directories is the local library, as the staff will often save the previous year's editions from all over the country if they are requested ahead of their expiration.

EXPLORING RESEARCH RESOURCE #7

Background

Wikipedia

While many students have been introduced to Wikipedia.org in their classrooms, they need to read entries with the understanding that in some cases, erroneous data has been placed there, intentionally or accidentally, so it is advised to confirm the information found there with at least one or two more stable sites. One of Wikipedia's interesting features is the site's interest in readers' submission to add to what its founder, Jimmy Wales, calls "the sum of all human knowledge." While the "–pedia" suffix of the word suggests an encyclopedic compilation, the beginning of the word, "wiki," comes from a shortened version of the Hawaiian term, wiki-wiki, which means "quick."

Activity

Many Internet users regard Wikipedia as the encyclopedia of Web users since everyone's input is both encouraged and used by the site. As an introductory assignment involving this site, challenge students to select a topic and research it on the Web in preparation for a submission to Wikipedia. For example, if students choose "intramural sports" as a topic, they must be able to locate information—either online, from magazines, or from their own experiences—to add to the existing entry on that topic. It's not as easy as it sounds. The Wikipedia.org site gets literally hundreds of submissions in a single day for a specific topic. The topics are as varied in range as the types of individuals who submit information. If students want to have a greater chance of submitting something unique to the site, they must be willing to venture into less familiar topics where their input may bring something new to the entry on that topic. Students may submit more than one item on the topic, but they must continue to submit until their input is accepted and posted.

From a different perspective, next allow students to select a topic to research using Wikipedia. Instruct them to review the submissions and use alternate sources to validate ten to twenty of the submissions. If, in the course of their search, they discover erroneous information, challenge them to find the correct information and submit it to the site for posting.

EXPLORING RESEARCH RESOURCE #8

Background

Encyclopedia

Despite the increased use of Internet resources, it is still important to familiarize students with standard volumes of encyclopedia. There will be instances when they are unable to access the Web and they should be able to locate information regardless of that fact. With little exposure to this reference, many students are not aware of how much and what kind of information is available to them in an encyclopedia. They may envision each volume as a "really large dictionary" with a lengthy definition and illustrations. They are often surprised to learn that, instead, in addition to providing a wealth of knowledge on a wide range of subjects, the encyclopedia is an ideal place to search for information that allows them to compare concepts they encounter in their subject area texts.

Activity

Specify a category, such as animals or transportation, and ask students to write, on separate index cards, several words that fit into that classification. Examples for the transportation category might include "car," "train," "airplane," "helicopter," "bus," "submarine," or "space shuttle." Collect the cards, divide the students into pairs, and give them two cards. Then write a list of eight to ten adjectives on the board, such as "big," "long," "young," "new," "expensive," "high," or "heavy." Instruct students to next use the encyclopedia to confirm comparisons between their two cards. For example, if the students are holding the cards, "car" and "helicopter," they can use encyclopedia entries to confirm that: (1) helicopters are newer than cars; (2) helicopters are more expensive than most cars; (3) cars are smaller than helicopters, and so on. Each pair should jot down their responses, along with the volume and page number of where they located their confirmation information.

The most organized method of searching in pairs is to have each team member focus on one of their words. For example, team member #1 can focus on the entry for the word, "car," while team member #2 finds as much as possible about the helicopter. In addition to improving research skills, this activity gives students an opportunity to work cooperatively with one another.

EXPLORING RESEARCH RESOURCE #9

Background

Atlas

Most of the maps that students encounter in the classrooms depict foreign lands they know only through their reading assignments or from some mention of them on the evening news. They often fail to make the connection between this type of map and the type their parents use to find their way on vacation. Unfortunately, the increased use of GPS for navigation purposes does not bode well for the development of map skills.

Children have a natural curiosity for anything they see being used by adults. They also have a vivid imagination and long to roam from familiar territory. By taking advantage of these two aspects of students' personalities, teachers can teach effective map skills and foster a willingness to use maps as reference materials.

Activity

Stop by a local AAA office to obtain maps of different states or of the entire United States. Bring the maps to class and talk about where students would like to visit in the fifty states, using the maps to plan routes and make travel arrangements. Students may work independently or in pairs to complete this activity.

Instruct students to plan a car trip from one state to another. (This portion of the assignment can also be a teacher-generated destination.) This trip must take students across at least two time zones. Challenge students to use their maps to answer the questions listed below. If working in pairs, designate one member of the team to keep track of the trip itinerary.

- *What is the starting point and destination of your trip?*
- *Through which states will you travel?*
- *How long will it take, traveling by car at 55 miles per hour for 12 hours per day? How many days will you be on the road before reaching your destination?*
- *Name three cities where you might stop to eat or stay for the night.*
- *What type of landforms (mountains, plains, deserts) will you experience during your trip?*
- *List three capital cities of states through which you'll travel even if your trip doesn't take you through that city.*

- *List three tourist attractions you would like to visit along the way.*
- *If you leave your watch on your home time zone, and it reads 4 P.M. when you arrive at your destination, what time is it in that city?*

Before beginning this or any other map activity, design exercises that require students to use a ruler and the map legends to determine distance between two cities. Do one or two activities together as a class before proceeding with individual or small group exercises.

EXPLORING RESEARCH RESOURCE #10

Background

Dictionary

Card games and worksheets that drill students on the correct use of guide words may set out to accomplish the same task, but the card game clearly has the advantage, not only in the area of built-in student motivation but also in providing a situation—one of playing cards with classmates during the school day, that beckons students to return for more practice. They become more proficient with guide words simply because they are investing more time working with them. In addition, students make choices on a strictly visual basis, which is a more realistic setting.

Activity

Create a list of thirty to fifty words beginning with the same initial letter ("city," "cat," "coat," "cell," "cost," etc.) and have students construct several decks of cards with one word on each card. More decks can be constructed with each deck containing thirty to fifty cards with the same initial letter (a "T" deck, a "J" deck, an "S" deck, etc). After the decks are constructed, divide students into three to four member groups giving each group its own deck of cards. Designate a dealer for each group who distributes five cards to each player then deals the next two cards face up on the table—these two cards are the guide words. To win the game, a player must hold five cards that fit correctly between the two guide words on the table, discarding all those words that do not fit. Players, in turn, draw and discard cards in an effort to build a winning hand. If no winner is declared by the time all cards on the deck have been drawn, players retain their cards, and the dealer shuffles the deck, drawing two new guide words. Play should then resume with the new guide words and continue until one player holds a winning hand even if the "redeal" process must be repeated. Also, allow students to rotate different decks (with different initial letters) so that they can become proficient at the recognition of guide words regardless of letter.

EXPLORING RESEARCH RESOURCE #11

Background

Atlas

Map skills may be a necessity beyond the classroom, yet many students still have no idea how to read a map or apply concept of scale, believing that based on proximity on a map, one can travel from New York City to Chicago by car during a lunch hour. Standardized test scores in this area help confirm this, showing insufficiencies in student knowledge and understanding of maps.

Maps follow the typical, alphabetical arrangement of most other reference materials. Before beginning any map activity, show students how to use map indicators printed in letters and numbers on the vertical and horizontal borders of a map as well as how to use a compass rose to locate specific places and make statements about how these locations relate to one another.

Activity

Students are more likely to become actively involved in an exercise if the topic is something they enjoy, such as sports. Below are sample questions for a map skills activity that students can complete individually or in pairs. Use a map of North America to locate answers to the questions listed below.

- *In what state do the Boston Celtics play their home games?*
- *If the Chicago Bears travel to their state's capital to receive an award from the governor, in what city will the ceremony take place?*
- *Which ocean is closest to the Seattle Mariners' home field?*
- *In which state do the San Francisco Giants and San Diego Padres play their home games?*
- *Name four states whose citizens might be New England Patriots' fans.*
- *Many games were played in Three Rivers Stadium in Pittsburgh. Name the three rivers represented by that title.*
- *If the Green Bay Packers are scheduled to meet the Denver Broncos in the Super Bowl, which team will travel the farthest to the stadium if the game is held in Indianapolis?*

Variations of this activity can be constructed using other popular culture topics, such as the touring schedule of a popular singer or group asking which capital cities the tour bus will travel through, and how many states the singer or group will visit throughout the tour.

EXPLORING RESEARCH RESOURCE #12

Background

Almanac

As newer methods for accessing information become available, students may have little or no idea of the value inherent in traditional reference resources that have been in use for many years. The almanac, in particular, contains a wealth of little known information on a variety of topics, including natural disasters, historical events, Olympic records, and other subject areas. Occasionally, a student will discover an almanac on a back shelf of the school library and spend the next several days pouring over the information contained between its covers. While the Almanac may never occupy the place of importance it held for our forefathers, its unique organization of information allows it to retain a certain attraction for learners of all ages.

Activity

This activity will work well for students studying state history. Write the names of states on individual index cards and place them in a bowl. Allow each student to draw a state name from the bowl. This state will then be the topic of an informal report using an almanac, compiling an interesting profile of the state to share with classmates. Students can select the information independently or respond to a group of questions you generate, such as the ones listed below.

- *What is the largest building in your state?*
- *What is the most populated city in your state?*
- *What is the yearly average of rainfall in your state?*
- *Name two famous people from your state.*
- *What states border your state?*
- *Name three major cities in your state.*
- *What is the main export or industry in your state?*
- *In the last three elections, what candidate did your state support?*
- *Name any presidents who were born in your state.*
- *Name any movies filmed on location in your state.*

Instruct students to compile their findings and present them to the class in a creative manner. The findings can be made into a brochure (using desktop software) or written on a pasteboard for a verbal in-class presentation. Other students may wish to compile a list to share with

classmates titled "Twenty Things You Might Not Know About
_____ ".

Variations of this assignment include giving students names of presidents, significant calendar years, or names of cities. In addition to learning more about this reference source, students have an opportunity to prepare a verbal presentation or create a brochure using desktop software.

EXPLORING RESEARCH RESOURCE #13

Background

Even as the Internet becomes a standard tool in classroom instruction and research, many students still have a somewhat antiquated method of looking for information that often proves time consuming and limited in appropriate return for their efforts. While there are many suitable search engines—www.google.com, www.dogpile.com, or www.ask.com—there are also a number of sites that contain information organized in an almanac format that are accessible especially for making comparisons between two or more events, objects, or trends. Introducing students to these sites may help them to become more effective researchers, saving themselves time and energy.

Activity

In recent years, almanacs have been less widely read or used as a form of research and information acquisition. They remain, however, a solid source of facts and compilations that can prove extremely helpful for several kinds of research projects.

Introduce students to these sites with a familiar game: the scavenger hunt. Provide students with the URL of some of the sites prior to distributing a list of items they must find online. More common almanac sites include www.libraryspot.com, www.refdesk.com, and www.educationindex.com, but there are numerous other sites that contain similar compilations of information. Working independently or in pairs, instruct students to log onto the Web and go on a scavenger hunt for the items listed on their worksheet. (It might be advisable to provide different search items for each team to reduce the possibility of answer sharing between pairs.) While speed is not critical while researching information, taking too long locating a single scrap of information may prove costly while chasing a research paper deadline. Here is a sample of the type of questions to use in such an activity, which can be substituted with a master list of teacher-created questions shared within a particular unit. Student teachers and parent volunteers can also be actively involved in developing a comprehensive list that can be rotated among classes. The purpose behind the activity is not the simple acquisition of information, but to provide students with a more effective method of locating the information.

- *Name the three longest rivers in the world.*
- *How many states contain a city named "Springfield?" Name them.*
- *What is "calamari" and where is it found?*
- *Who was the nation's thirteenth president? Where was he born?*
- *How many women have served in the U.S. Congress? Name them.*
- *Which is taller: The Sears Tower or the Transamerica Building? By how many feet? In what state is each building located?*
- *Which state capital is most densely populated? Which world capital?*
- *What is the definition of a "peninsula?" Name three peninsulas.*

CHAPTER EIGHT

Improving Study and Test-Taking Skills

The most important part of teaching is to teach what it is "to know."

—Simone Weil

Many students perform poorly on tests not because of a lack of knowledge of the subject matter, but rather a lack of basic understanding of how to prepare for and take written examinations. In many instances, these students are active participants during classroom discussions about the topic, yet when faced with a written testing instrument, their inability to deal with the format hinders their overall scores. Fortunately, there are a number of strategies that teachers can share with students to overcome these challenges and reduce test anxiety.

Managing pretesting and testing situations means taking advantage of available notes and study aids. Chapter 5 contains information about effective note taking and organization. Chapter 7 offers advice about how to access relevant information to develop a clearer understanding of content area topics. In this chapter, strategies will be presented incorporating the information from those chapters as they pertain to test preparation and performance.

In a modern school setting, many examinations are government mandated and do not relate to a specific topic from class textbooks, so performance cannot be enhanced with the aid of a unit study guide. These proficiency tests remain a part of the educational landscape for today's students and teachers, and some of the information in this chapter can be applied successfully to these instruments.

While the majority of teachers prefer not to "teach to the test," there are some strategies they can employ in planning and presenting units of study that will encourage students to connect the new material to what they already know about a specific topic. Fostering this relationship between new and previously learned information is a critical step in genuine understanding of subject matter and long-term retention of a concept.

USING THIS CHAPTER

As greater emphasis is placed on students and teachers regarding test performance, it is critical to provide students with the tools they need to become competent test takers. These strategies not only include improving student study skills but also adopting pretest behaviors that will maximize performance. And while teachers loathe the notion of "teaching to the test," the mounting pressure on the educational community leads to a need for restructuring the methods used to prepare students to take examinations.

While some of the strategies offered in this chapter involve student behaviors in pretest and posttest settings, other activities seek to help teachers bring a more test-wise student population to the examination room.

Finally, this chapter offers tips and techniques to improve students' study skills for nonstandardized evaluations by teaching them to identify critical information in their reading assignments.

IMPROVING STUDY AND TEST-TAKING SKILLS #1

Background

Test preparation begins the instant the teacher introduces a unit of study to the class. It is at this point that learners must decide how to organize the information they will be receiving during the unit. Their goals should include long-term retention of the material as well as how this new information relates to what they already know about the topic. As test day approaches, students who have invested the time and energy in reviewing the material and made use of supplemental resources will need to make only minor adjustments to their daily routine to prepare for the examination.

Activity

Within the first few weeks of the school year, it is important to begin discussing test preparation with students. In addition to the standardized tests, each grade requires a specific level of mastery in a variety of subjects. By setting guidelines early in the year, students and teacher can work together to reduce some of the anxiety that accompanies the testing situation. Use some of the questions listed here to guide this discussion.

- *How does knowing the test format beforehand help you prepare for it?*
- *Name three ways you can make your notes more useful when studying for examinations.*
- *What study aids do you think would be most helpful if the test has a multiple-choice format? True or false? Fill in the blanks?*
- *Why do you think that teachers recommend skipping over test questions you can't answer, returning to them later in the testing session?*
- *Name three ways that having a study buddy might affect your performance on an examination.*
- *Why should you ask teachers beforehand to identify the test format? Explain your response.*
- *What effect do you think regular note review will have on your test preparation and performance?*
- *Can you think of a reason for creating mock questions that match the test format to use while studying for an examination?*
- *Name three things not related to studying that you could do the day before the test to improve your performance. Explain your response.*

IMPROVING STUDY AND TEST-TAKING SKILLS #2

Background

Many times, students know the material being covered on tests but are uncertain about the definition of the terms used on test questions. For example, a student may possess sufficient knowledge about simple machines but does not understand the term, "evaluate," and misses the question that requires students to "compare simple machines and evaluate which one has the greatest impact on daily life." Pretesting activities that help students become familiar with this type of testing terminology will likely maximize student performance on tests, allowing them to state what they know about a topic using the specified format.

Activity

There are a number of terms that are used consistently in standardized testing formats. Activities that create opportunities for students to use these terms, sometimes referred to as *process verbs*, with familiar material will allow them to become proficient at performing the desired task. Listed below are some of the more common process verbs followed by some suggested activities for familiarizing students with their proper use.

- *Analyze: to separate an entity into parts for closer examination*
- *Infer: to draw a conclusion based on facts and/or information*
- *Synthesize: to form a new entity from various parts or elements*
- *Evaluate: to rate or rank based on a set of criteria*
- *Predict: to make educated guesses about what will occur*

Analyze

Begin with a concrete object, such as a desk or shoe. Challenge students to examine the object and list as many components as possible. Follow this exercise with a discussion of which components seem to be the most critical (i.e., a desk needs a writing surface and legs) and which components are less essential (i.e., fancy detailing on a tennis shoe does not affect its durability). Then move onto a written composition, employing the same technique. In a business letter, for example, what are the individual components and which ones cannot be eliminated? Which elements can be reduced or omitted without serious consequence?

Infer

Show students a short video or read a short written passage aloud. The video or passage should involve traditional behaviors of any species, from humans to hippos. Ask students to watch the video or listen to the passage, using the information shared to draw a conclusion about the species. For instance, "All the hippos in the video seemed to stay in or near the water so it could be inferred that hippos prefer being wet to being dry;" or, a written passage about frequent cell phone users failing to interact with people around them might lead to the inference that cell phones are actually decreasing our ability to communicate with people in close proximity to us. Follow the illustrations with a discussion about what elements in the video or written passage led to the stated inferences.

Synthesize

Dismantle three to four existing art projects or room decorations, placing students in small groups charged with the challenge to create some new and hopefully more useful items from the component parts of these objects. For example, some flowers from a spring room display might be attached to the front of a student-made Mother's Day card to increase its size and improve its overall appearance. Once the items are compiled, discuss what thought processes went into the decision of which components parts were used to construct the new object.

Evaluate

Display an array of three to five objects that are used daily in the classroom, such as books or writing instruments. Ask students to determine a set of criteria for what makes the object desirable. For instance, a book is easy to read, has great characters and colorful pictures. Next, have students evaluate the books on display. Which book is the best based on the set of criteria? Afterwards, discuss how students decided on which criteria were of greatest or least importance in determining if a book was (or wasn't) a good book.

Predict

Read aloud (or allow students to read independently) a portion of a book stopping at a significant event. Then, ask students to predict what they think will happen next. Keep the questions open-ended and encourage students to reflect on what earlier events in the story influenced their responses. Follow with a discussion about the impact that predicting has on students' ability to understand what is coming next in the story.

IMPROVING STUDY AND TEST-TAKING SKILLS #3

Background

Athletes try to take good care of their bodies—even in the off season. In this way, they ensure that their transition from semi-idle to full action is smooth and effortless. Similarly, those students who develop a test-taking perspective view new information as it might appear in a future quiz or test. This mentality allows them to hear, then discard, meaningless details, retaining more valuable information relating to processes and term definitions.

Adopting testing behaviors during the *off season*—between exams— enables students to spring into full action when testing time arrives, and the *big game* is on the line. Developing and maintaining positive study habits throughout the school year makes unproductive cramming before a test unnecessary. Helping students learn to develop some of the following test-preparation and test-taking strategies will greatly reduce typical test day anxiety for everyone as students enter the testing situation feeling relaxed and confident that they can get the job done.

Activity

Teachers modeling organized behaviors are more likely to have organized students. Discuss the strategies listed here to set students up for success. If students can make the connection between ample preparation and improved performance, they are more likely to invest the time and effort in adopting these strategies. As these strategies are presented, encourage student feedback. Knowing what students are thinking is key to helping them see the value of changing poor habits in studying and test taking.

- *Arrive on time for the test. If you feel anxious or hurried, you won't do your best work.*
- *Read as much of the test as you are allowed before beginning to familiarize yourself with the information being requested.*
- *Follow all written and oral directions carefully and don't be afraid to ask for clarification of instructions before the test begins.*
- *Bring a sufficient number of writing instruments to the testing setting as well as any other materials you are permitted, such as a calculator or scratch paper.*

- *After gaining teacher permission, write all that you know on the back of your test before beginning. This "brain dump" will let you relax, as you won't be trying to retain all the information at one time.*
- *Do the easy questions first—return for the more difficult ones later.*
- *Complete objective questions before essay questions. Some facts in the multiple choice or matching items might help you answer the essays.*
- *Save questions you're unsure of until the end of the test. Don't waste precious time rereading them over and over.*
- *Unless you'll be penalized, guess on the questions you simply can't answer. You may be storing some subconscious material on the topic and be able to make an educated guess.*
- *Answer all test questions before turning in your paper or booklet.*

IMPROVING STUDY AND TEST-TAKING SKILLS #4

Background

Before taking a standardized test, it is helpful to allow students to practice working with the test format. So that students are able to focus primarily on the format, a practice test containing items that mirror the standardized test format but using material that is extremely familiar can be an excellent tool. Dropping back one grade level is also helpful, along with developing questions that have some of the process verbs commonly used in standardized tests. Using the more familiar information will allow students to deal more with the test format and less with the actual information.

Activity

Begin by creating an environment that replicates the standardized testing setting as closely as possible. Write a set of directions similar to what students encounter on those tests, and construct an answer sheet that resembles those papers used in actual testing situations. The key factor for this exercise is to put students in the mindset they will need to perform on a standardized test.

The difference in this exercise is that the material on this mock test will be at least one grade level below what the students will encounter on the actual examination. Since students are already very familiar with the material being requested in the test questions, they can focus their energies on the actual test completion process as well as practice some testing behaviors such as reading the test first and responding to easier questions before more difficult items.

Designate a day as "test day" and have students behave as they do when standardized tests are administered. Use any required components (#2 pencils, calculators, etc.) that are used on the actual test day. Avoid referring to this occasion as a "mock" or "fake" test. The more closely the testing environment is copied, the increased likelihood it will elicit an appropriate student response.

Participating in a simulation activity provides students with an opportunity to build their confidence for the actual event. Using test items that are more familiar to students allows them to focus on the test instrument itself and on how to correctly complete the answer sheet. Another change might be to include popular culture questions that are of interest to students. Again, the primary focus will be on filling out the test instrument correctly. Following the test, review the experience with students encouraging their feedback about how they felt during the testing situation. Additionally, discuss other ways that anxiety can be reduced on test day such as doing something enjoyable as a group before and/or after the test.

IMPROVING STUDY AND TEST-TAKING SKILLS #5

Background

Matching tests are most commonly used to test such areas as vocabulary, states and capitals, and famous people and their achievements. Based on simple recall, these tests do not require students to discuss the information as it relates to other concepts in the unit of study.

Since matching tests are a recall exercise, one of the most effective ways to prepare for a matching test is through the use of flash cards. While there are commercially prepared cards available on a variety of subjects, allowing students to make their own cards provides one more opportunity for the students to review the material as they organize and copy it onto the cards. By deciding what information will go on the cards, students must sift through facts and figures in a purposeful search that is also a mini review session.

Activity

Allow students to work in pairs for this activity. While sharing the type of information that will be contained on an upcoming test, ask students to identify which information might be well suited for flash card review. Dates and events, names and achievements, terms and definitions, and English and foreign words are only a few of the categories that work well with this study format.

Instruct students to work with their texts, notes, and any other supplemental material (field trip brochures, guest speaker information) that will be included on the test. Have the group brainstorm for a list of names, a list of terms, or a set of dates. This list can be copied on one side of the flash cards, one name, term, or date per card. On the opposite side of each card, have students write achievements, definitions, or events that correspond with the information on the front of the card. Encourage students to use these cards while working with their study buddies during independent time in class.

On test day, encourage students to cover the left hand column of the matching items and read the right hand column (the column that contains the achievement, definition, or event) first, answering as many items as possible without assistance from the left-hand column. Having the answer to these items without looking up and down the left-hand column saves valuable test taking time that can be used on other parts of the examination.

If the matching test involves vocabulary terms, look for parts of speech contained in the definition; for example, a definition that begins with "a group of" most likely refers to a noun and "the act of" is defining a verb. Prefixes and suffixes may also hold the key to word meaning.

IMPROVING STUDY AND TEST-TAKING SKILLS #6

Background

True or false tests measure the learner's recognition of factual statements. Remind students that although, in most cases, statements are phrased as simple declarative sentences, they may sometimes contain trick words such as "always" or "never." Since absolutes rarely exist in the real world, students need to be aware of statements that contain these markers.

Activities

Prior to administering a true or false test to students, take time to review some information about these statements. A *true* statement is only true if 100 percent of the statement is true; a *false* statement may contain truths but it is not completely true and is, therefore, a false statement.

Instruct students, working independently, to review the major topics being covered on the test and write five to seven statements that are true about the topic. Moving beyond simply reading the text to actually generating and writing a list of true statements enhances the review process greatly. Next have students exchange lists with a classmate challenging that student to substitute one word that will make the sentence false.

Another effective review method for true or false statements is to reduce the statements to a basic *subject/predicate/object* framework for clarity of meaning. For example, in the sentence, "Thomas Jefferson, one of the chief architects of the Declaration of Independence and a powerful supporter of independence from the English crown, served as the fourth president of the United States." Reducing this sentence to a basic framework of subject/predicate/object reveals that "Thomas Jefferson served as the fourth president of the United States." While much of the other information in the statement is true, the fact remains that Jefferson was the third president so the statement is false.

After exhausting all other means of completing a true or false statement, let students know that it's okay to guess—unless they will be penalized. The odds of correctly responding to a true or false statement are, after all, one chance in two.

IMPROVING STUDY AND TEST-TAKING SKILLS #7

Background

In addition to their use for basic recall of factual material, multiple-choice questions often ask a student to identify relationships that exist among concepts being presented in a unit of study. Therefore, the learner's depth of knowledge of the topic must run a little deeper than simple recall. This role of multiple-choice questions can be discussed with students, reminding them that once again, it is a good idea to look for absolutes such as "always" or "never" since these absolutes rarely exist in reality.

Activity

Demonstrate these study strategies in class to help students prepare for their next multiple-choice test. This activity works well with a study buddy who can check answers for accuracy. Begin by writing test topics on colored index cards. Then, on plain white cards, write at least five statements about each topic. Instruct students to shuffle all white cards and try to place them under the corresponding topic card. On the back of the cards, write the correct test topic for self-checking after completing the activity. This activity can also work well for students to complete during an independent period.

During a multiple-choice test, remind students to read each option—A, B, C, and D—as four complete statements. Thinking of each of the statements as a complete thought makes it easier to recognize the correct response (or responses in the case of an "all of the above" option). Share the example below with students to demonstrate how to separate one multiple-choice test item into four separate statements.

The *protagonist* of a story

    (a) is always a man

    (b) never does anything evil

    (c) is usually a sympathetic character

    (d) wants to destroy the antagonist

Read the possible responses as follows:

    (a) The *protagonist* of a story is always a man.

    (b) The *protagonist* of a story never does anything evil.

(c)   The *protagonist* of a story is usually a sympathetic character.

(d)   The *protagonist* of a story wants to destroy the antagonist.

Choice A can be eliminated because there are many female protagonists in stories.

Choice B is unlikely because humans have shortcomings and are capable of evil.

Choice D is also unlikely because the protagonist is often trying to save the antagonist from himself or herself.

Choice C is the most likely option; the statement is not an absolute, as it contains the term, "usually" and the protagonist, the story's hero(ine) often falls into that category. So, choice C is the logical choice.

References

Chapman, C., & King, R. (2003). *Differentiated instructional strategies for reading in the content areas.* Thousand Oaks, CA: Corwin Press.

Graves, M., & Graves, B. (1994). *Scaffolding reading experiences.* Norwood, MA: Christopher-Gordon Publishers.

Maccagnano, A. (2007). *Identifying and enhancing the strengths of gifted learners.* Thousand Oaks, CA: Corwin Press.

Ogle, D. (1986). K-W-L: A teaching model that develops active reading of expository text. *The Reading Teacher, 39,* 564–571.

Pauk, W. (2000). *How to study in college* (7th ed.). Boston: Houghton Mifflin.

Richardson, W. (2006). *Blogs, wikis, podcasts, and other powerful Web tools for the classroom.* Thousand Oaks, CA: Corwin Press.

Snow, A. P., & Sweet, C. E. (Eds.). (2003). *Rethinking reading comprehension.* New York: Guilford.

Index

CORWIN
PRESS

The Corwin Press logo—a raven striding across an open book—represents the union of courage and learning. Corwin Press is committed to improving education for all learners by publishing books and other professional development resources for those serving the field of PreK–12 education. By providing practical, hands-on materials, Corwin Press continues to carry out the promise of its motto: **"Helping Educators Do Their Work Better."**